pilgrim
GUIDE
du pèlerin

17th World Youth Day
17e Journée mondiale de la jeunesse

Toronto Canada
July 18-28 juillet 2002

ENGLISH FRANÇAIS ESPAÑOL ITALIANO

NOVALIS

EMERGENCY NUMBERS

- In case of an emergency, find a telephone and dial 911.
- For all other information needs, call the World Youth Day Info Hotline at (416) 913-2080 or ask at a WYD Info Booth.

NUMÉROS DE SECOURS

- En cas d'urgence, trouvez un téléphone et composez le 911.
- Pour toute autre information, appelez la Ligne Info de la Journée mondiale de la jeunesse au (416) 913-2080 ou adressez votre demande à un Kiosque Info de la JMJ.

NÚMEROS DE EMERGENCIA

- En caso de emergencia, busca un teléfono y marca 911
- Para obtener cualquier otro tipo de información, llama a la Línea de Información de la Jornada Mundial de la Juventud al (416) 913-2080 o dirígete a una Cabina de Información de la JMJ.

NUMERI D'EMERGENZA

- In caso d'emergenza, trovate un telefono e componete il 911.
- Per qualsiasi altra informazione, chiamate la Info Line della Giornata Mondiale della Gioventù al (416) 913-2080 oppure rivolgetevi ad un Info Point della GMG.

الارقام الاضطرارية

- في الحالات الاضطرارية، استعينوا بالهاتف واتصلوا بالرقم: (911).
- للحصول على المعلومات الضرورية الاخرى، اتصلوا برقم هاتف مركزمعلومات اليوم العالمي للشباب المباشر والمستعجل التالي: 913-2080 (416) او اسألوا مركز معلومات اليوم العالمي للشباب.

NOTFALL NUMMERN

- Im Falle eines Notfalls, finde ein Telefon und wähle 911
- Für jeden weiteren Bedarf an Information, rufe die Weltjugendtags Hotline an unter (416) 913-2080 oder frage bei einem WYD Info Stand.

SEGÉLYHÍVÓ TELEFONSZÁMOK

- Szükséghelyzetben keress egy telefont, és hívd a 911-en a rendőrséget /a tűzoltóságot /a mentőket!
- Egyéb segítsért vagy tájékotatásért hívd a 416 913-2080 as WYD információs közvetlen vonalat, vagy keresd fel a „WYD Info Booth" felirattal ellátott helyeket!

NUMERY AWARYJNE

- W razie wypadku należy telefonować pod numer 911.
- W celu uzyskania wszelkich innych informacji należy telefonować pod numer (416) 913-2080, będący specjalną linią informacyjną Krajowego Biura Organizacyjnego Światowego Dnia Młodzieży w Toronto lub zgłosić się do punktu informacyjnego ŚDM.

NÚMEROS DE EMERGÊNCIA

- Em caso de emergência, ligue para o número 911.
- Para maiores informações, ligue para a Central de Informações do Dia Mundial da Juventude no número (416) 913-2080 ou dirija-se a um quiosque de informações do DMJ.

NUMERE DE URGENȚĂ

- In caz de urgență, găsiți un telefon și formați 911.
- Pentru orice altă informație, sunați la Centrul de Informare al World Youth Day la (416) 913-2080 sau întrebați la Chioșcul de informații (WYD Info Booth).

Номера Телефонів Допомоги

- У випадку крайньої потреби, знайдіть телефон та набиріть номер 911.
- При потребі будь-якої іншої інформації, дзвоніть до довідкового бюра Світового Дня Молоді по телефону, (416) 913-2080, або звертайтеся до їхніх кіосків.

CÁC SỐ ĐIỆN THOẠI KHI CẦN

- Trường hợp khẩn cấp, xin gọi 911

- Cần biết mọi chi tiết khác, xin gọi World Youth Day Info Hotline (416) 913-2080 hoặc đến Quầy Thông Tin WYD

KAPAG NANGAILANGAN NG TULONG O MAY 'EMERGENCY' :

- Sa oras ng matinding pangangailangan, maghanap ng telepono at tumawag sa numero 911.
- Para sa iba pang informasyon, tawagan ang World Youth Day Info Hotline sa numero (416) 913-2080 o' magtanong sa mga nakatalagang WYD Info Booth.

緊急電話號碼

- 緊急情況時，請找尋電話，撥 911。

- 如有其他消息需要，請撥世青熱線 416-913-2080 或在世青詢問處查詢。

비상시 전화

- 비상시에는 가까운 곳의 전화를 찾아서 911 번으로 전화
- 다른 정보의 필요를 위해서는 세계 청소년 대회 안내 전화 (416) 913-2080 으로 전화하거나 또는 세계 청소년 대회 안내소에 질문하기 바람

ENGLISH

TABLE OF CONTENTS

SYMBOLS

Garbage/Recycling

Pilgrim Hospital First Aid

Regional/City Hospital

Security

Registration

Drinking Water

Non-potable Water

Pilgrim Food

Toilets

Information

Food to Purchase

Toilets Men

Bus/Bus stop

TAXI

Special Needs Meeting Place

Toilets Women

Stage

Wheelchair Accessible

Shops

Danger Electricity

Wheelchair Accessible with Assistance

Lost and Found

Pay Attention

Special Needs Reserved Viewing Area

Telephone

BÉNÉVOLE WTD2002JMJ VOLUNTEER

Wheelchair Accessible Toilets

Meeting Place & Lost Pilgrims

Toronto Transit Commission

Special Needs Rest Area

Internet

Transit GO Transit

HEALTH

If You Need Medical Help

In a medical emergency, call 911 at any time and from any location.

This number can be dialled free from any telephone. Inform the Emergency Services operator that you are a WYD participant and provide your location. The operator will help you with appropriate instructions.

At WYD Sites

- Alert any WYD volunteer or paramedic. Volunteers wearing a red shirt with a white cross are trained health care providers.
- Go to the nearest WYD health care station, marked by a white cross inside a red circle.

Throughout Toronto

- Tell your group leader or billeting host, and they will direct you to the nearest medical centre.
- Always take someone with you when you seek medical help.
- When you go to a clinic or hospital, tell the medical staff that you are a WYD participant.
- Always carry your insurance number with you. Keep your medical receipts.

Safety in the Sun and Heat

Summer in Toronto can be extremely hot and humid. To protect yourself from the sun and heat:

- Wear a hat and look for shaded areas or create shade using an umbrella.
- Wear clothing that protects as much of your skin as possible.
- Wear sunglasses that have UVA and UVB protection.

- Use sunscreen with a sun protection factor (SPF) of 15 or higher. Re-apply every two to three hours.
- Dress in layers to adapt to varying temperatures throughout the day.
- Drink plenty of water and carry a bottle of water with you at all times.
- Toronto's tap water is safe to drink. Bottled water is also widely available.

Toronto's Smoking and Drinking Laws

- The legal drinking age in Toronto, and throughout Ontario, is 19. Consumption of alcohol is not permitted outside bars and restaurants except in designated patio areas.
- To buy cigarettes or other tobacco products, you must be 19 years of age.
- Smoking is not permitted inside schools or on school grounds or inside most public buildings. Before lighting up in public places, find out if smoking is permitted.
- Many Toronto restaurants are smoke-free; only those with a designated fully enclosed smoking room permit smoking. Smoking is permitted In bars, unless otherwise noted. Restaurants that allow unenclosed smoking are not permitted to admit customers who are under 19.

Other Health Tips

- Occasional *smog alerts* may be called by the City of Toronto's public health department to indicate poor air quality. If you have asthma, allergies, or a heart or lung condition, you need to take special care not to overexert yourself. Pace your activity, keep cool and drink plenty of water. If you feel unwell, seek medical attention.
- All Toronto beaches are posted with signs indicating whether it is safe to swim. Some swimming areas are unsupervised. Always swim with a friend and follow the posted rules.

- If you are bitten or scratched by an animal, notify your group leader, billeting host or a WYD staff member or volunteer. Wash the wound with soap and warm water and clean thoroughly. Seek medical attention.

PILGRIMS WITH SPECIAL NEEDS

WYD events, ceremonies and celebrations have been planned and organized to include people with special needs whenever possible. Event sites also display internationally recognized symbols to assist and direct persons with special needs.

Special Needs Transportation

WYD has made every effort to ensure transportation to events is available for mobility-impaired pilgrims. Pilgrims with mobility impairments will need to arrange their own transportation to non-WYD outings. Accessible transportation options include: Wheel-Trans (416) 393-4222; Royal Taxi Services (416) 955-0564; Beck Taxi (416) 751-5555; TPT (416) 209-0950; and Able Atlantic Taxi (416) 291-4363.

STAYING SAFE

Toronto is among the world's safest cities, but travellers should always exercise caution in unfamiliar settings.

Personal Safety

- Whenever possible, travel in groups and use the buddy system.
- Walk confidently and be aware of your surroundings at all times.
- Walk in well-lit areas, preferably on the same side of the road as the streetlights.
- After dark, avoid shortcuts through vacant lots, alleyways, parks or school yards.

- If you suspect that you are being followed, go to the nearest public area and call the police by dialling **911**.
- In bars or dance clubs, *never* leave your drink unattended or accept pills from anyone.

Keeping Your Belongings Safe

- Personalize your WYD knapsack and other bags with items you can easily recognize. This can include the flag of your country, collector patches or distinctive coloured material.
- Place luggage tags on the inside and outside of your knapsack and other bags. Record only your name and country of origin on the tags; do not include personal information. Use luggage locks to keep zippered pouches secure.
- Place name tags on clothing items.
- Keep prescription drugs with you at all times.
- Do not carry large amounts of cash; use traveller's cheques or credit cards whenever possible. A waist pouch is safer than a purse or wallet.
- Never leave your belongings unattended, particularly at the airport, or at bus or train stations.
- Whenever possible, leave travel documents and valuables secure where you are staying. Do not bring them to event sites.
- Photocopy all important travel documents such as passports and airline tickets. Record the serial numbers of your traveller's cheques and electronic equipment, and the account numbers of your credit cards. Immediately report lost or stolen travel or personal documents to police or to a volunteer who can direct you to the nearest police officer.

Fire Safety

To reduce the risk of fire:

- Open flames, including lit candles, are forbidden in all areas of your accommodations.
- Keep burning candles away from flammable materials and never leave candles unattended.
- If you observe potential fire hazards, call (416) 338-9050.

If you discover a fire:

- Leave the area immediately and help anyone in danger to leave.
- Activate the fire alarm and alert staff.
- Follow the instructions listed below.

If you hear a fire alarm in a building:

- Obey instructions from building staff.
- Leave the building immediately.
- Close all doors behind you.
- Use stairwells to leave the building. Do not use elevators.
- Proceed to designated outside assembly area. Do not re-enter the building.

LOST OR STOLEN PASSPORT OR VISA

You must report lost or stolen passports to the nearest police station. You should also contact your country's consulate or embassy to report the loss and to obtain a replacement. The list of Embassies and Consulates at the back of this book contains the information you need to contact officials from your country.

LOST AND FOUND

The Toronto Police Service will operate Lost and Found offices at Exhibition Place and Downsview Lands. You may report a loss or turn over a found item at these locations.

YOUR KNAPSACK

Inside your knapsack you will find:
- a map of Toronto
- WYD pin
- WYD bandanna
- candles
- cup to hold candles
- cross
- rosary
- Canada pin
- Canadian flag
- luggage tags
- postcards

Note: When you receive your knapsack, you will also be given the Liturgy Book, the Pilgrim Guide and your Pass.

YOUR PASS

- Your Pass allows you to participate in all WYD events. It also enables you to use Toronto's public transportation system at no cost during WYD.
- Please fill in the Pass with the important details requested. You will find WYD emergency and information numbers on the Pass.
- Please make WYD a success by wearing your Pass in clear view at all times.
- The coloured border on your Pass matches the colour of your assigned section at Downsview Lands.
- If you lose your Pass, go to a WYD Info Booth or registration centre for help.

APPROPRIATE BEHAVIOUR

While you are in Toronto, your behaviour reflects on all Catholic young people. If you show offensive behaviour that disrupts the conduct of official activities, you will be removed.

ACCOMMODATION

At each WYD housing facility, trained teams are available to help you. These volunteers are your hosts. Follow all safety instructions and report any concerns you have to them.

Schools and Other Group Accommodation

- You will always need to present your Pass to enter your accommodations.

- Respect the arrival and departure times given by the hosting teams. WYD housing sites are open from 8:00 p.m. to 9:00 a.m. Facilities are locked at all other times and no one will be admitted. If you become ill and are unable to attend the day's activities, you will be directed to the nearest WYD infirmary.

- Please use public areas only and keep noise levels to a minimum in the sleeping areas. Refrain from disruptive behaviour and respect your fellow pilgrims' right to privacy and to peace and quiet.

- Smoking and the consumption of alcoholic beverages are strictly prohibited in or on any of the WYD accommodation properties. If you break these rules, you will be removed from the property immediately and you will have to make other accommodation arrangements at your own expense.

- The use of electric appliances or equipment, such as kettles or heating devices, is prohibited.

- Facilities are locked at 1:00 a.m. Please return to accommodation sites before this time.

- All food must be consumed outside the properties. No meals are permitted indoors.

Family Homes

- Staying in a family home is a privilege. Please respect the hosts who have welcomed you into their homes.

- Please obey your host's house rules and requests concerning such matters as curfews and departure times.

GETTING AROUND TORONTO

Toronto is a very easy city for visitors to travel around, and most Torontonians are happy to provide directions. Ask for help if you are lost or confused.

Public Transportation

- The Toronto Transit Commission (TTC) operates buses, streetcars and subway service throughout the city. GO Transit operates train and bus service in the Greater Toronto Area (GTA). Local transit service is also available in the areas surrounding the GTA.
  - For TTC service information, call (416) 393-4636
  - For GO information, call (416) 869-3200

- Your registration provides free passage on the TTC for the dates identified on your registration. For TTC travel outside of these dates, regular TTC fares apply.

- When riding the subway, buses or streetcars, please remember these safety tips:
  - On buses, "Request Stop" allows women travelling alone between 9:00 p.m. and 5:00 a.m. to ask the driver to let them off between stops.
  - When leaving streetcars, look to the right before stepping onto the street. Make sure all traffic has stopped.
  - Designated Waiting Areas are located on all subway/ Rapid Transit (RT) platforms. These areas are well lit and have an intercom that connects to TTC station staff.
  - Passenger Assistance Alarms are on all subway/RT

cars. Press this alarm to report fire, harassment, illness, accidents, vandalism, or any incident affecting passenger safety.

Taxis

- In downtown Toronto, it is easy to flag a taxi on the street. If a car's roof light is on, it is available. To call a taxi, please consult the Yellow Pages telephone directory and look under *Taxis*.

- Make sure that the meter is on before your ride begins. Pay the amount indicated by the meter; tipping is optional.

- Although taxi service is widely available in Toronto, it can be expensive. A trip from downtown to the outer suburbs is costly. You can ask the taxi company dispatcher or the driver to quote you an approximate fare before you decide to ride.

- All Toronto taxis require the driver and vehicle to be licensed. The driver's photo and the taxi owner's information must be posted in the taxi on the back of the headrests. For complaints and information, call 1-877-868-2947.

Parking on Toronto Streets or Private Property

- Parking in Toronto is *strictly* enforced by police and parking authorities and fines are costly. To avoid having your vehicle towed, obey all signs and do not leave your car on any property unless it is a designated parking location.

- If you park at a parking lot without an attendant, follow the posted rules.

- For information or complaints regarding parking, call (416) 392-3082.

Driving in Toronto

- For road information, call (416) 599-9090.

- There is no vehicle access to Exhibition Place and Downsview Lands during WYD.

EVENT LOCATIONS

Note that two-way radios and walkie-talkie-type radios are prohibited at all sites and will be disabled once detected. Please use cellular telephones when you need to communicate.

Exhibition Place

Exhibition Place, located near downtown Toronto just north of Lake Ontario, is open from 9:00 a.m. to 10:00 p.m. from Monday, July 22 to Thursday, July 25, and from 9:00 a.m. to 6:00 p.m. on Friday, July 26.

Exhibition Place is the location of catecheses from Wednesday, July 24 to Friday, July 26. In the afternoons, a nearby area, Duc in Altum Park, is available for the Sacrament of Reconciliation. During the afternoons and evenings, Exhibition Place also hosts the Youth Festival.

All participants come to Exhibition Place for the **Papal Welcoming Ceremony** at 5:00 p.m. on Thursday, July 25.

Note that the following items and activities are prohibited at Exhibition Place:

- propane
- barbecues
- camping
- roller blades
- bicycles
- scooters
- skateboards
- glass bottles
- alcoholic beverages
- fireworks

Anything in your possession may be searched.

University Avenue

University Avenue is one of the main streets of Toronto. At 7:30 p.m. on Friday, July 26, the **Way of the Cross** ceremony will begin at Nathan Phillips Square, in front of Toronto City Hall. It will continue north on University Avenue, past the Legislature of the Province of Ontario and the University of Toronto, ending at the Royal Ontario Museum, near the intersection of Bloor Street West and Avenue Road.

Downsview Lands

Pilgrims will converge at Downsview Lands in northwest Toronto, 15 km from Exhibition Place, on Saturday, July 27. Please note that you will *not* be allowed into Downsview Lands before 8:00 a.m. on Saturday, July 27. You will be assigned one of four walking routes, each about 8 km.

You will participate in a **Vigil with the Pope,** which will include prayers, songs, scripture readings, testimonies and a message from the Pope, beginning at 7:30 p.m. on July 27. Following the Vigil, the Pope will depart for the night and you will sleep outside at Downsview Lands.

On Sunday, July 28, the Pope will celebrate Mass at 9:30 a.m. to conclude WYD. The Mass is open to members of the public. Please remain on site for at least one hour after the **Papal Mass,** so that the members of the public have an opportunity to leave first. WYD also requests that you clean up litter and deposit it in appropriate collection bins or bags that will be provided. You *must* leave Downsview Lands by 9:00 p.m. on July 28.

Note that all items and activities forbidden at Exhibition Place are also forbidden at Downsview Lands, with the exception of camping overnight on Saturday, July 27.

MEALS

Full Meal Plan

The full meal plan includes 11 meals, beginning with supper on Tuesday, July 23 and ending with lunch on Sunday, July 28.

Weekend Meal Plan

The weekend meal plan covers three meals: supper on Saturday, July 27 and breakfast and lunch on Sunday, July 28.

The Menus

Menus reflect a wide range of cuisine from a variety of cultures. Of the 11 meals in the full meal program, eight feature a hot entrée. Cold boxed meals are provided so that you can attend events throughout the city without having to return to your meal station.

The menu is based on Canada's Food Guide to Healthy Eating and meets required nutritional guidelines.

A vegetarian offering is available at each meal.

Food Times and Locations

Meal pavilions are located at both Exhibition Place and Downsview Lands. Your meal station is based on your assigned catechesis location.

Tuesday, July 23

- **Supper** is served after the Opening Mass of Welcome, approximately 6:30 p.m., and continues until 10:00 p.m.

Wednesday, July 24

- **Lunch** starts after the catecheses, approximately 12:30 p.m., and continues until 2:30 p.m.
- **Supper** starts at 5:30 p.m. and continues until 8:00 p.m.

Thursday, July 25

- **Lunch** starts after the catecheses, approximately 12:30

p.m., and continues until 2:30 p.m.

- **Supper** will be served at Exhibition Place following the Papal Welcoming Ceremony, from 6:30 p.m. until 10:00 p.m.

Friday, July 26

- **Lunch** begins after the catecheses, approximately 12:30 p.m., and continues until 2:30 p.m.
- A cold **boxed supper** is available at your assigned meal station for pickup during the lunch hour to allow everyone to participate in the Way of the Cross.

Saturday, July 27

- A **boxed lunch** is distributed to pilgrims along their assigned pilgrimage route from 8:30 a.m. to 4:00 p.m.

Food Service at Downsview Lands

The meal plan at Downsview Lands, including the Weekend Meal Plan, covers the following three meals:

Saturday, July 27

- **Supper** starts at 4:00 p.m. and continues until 7:00 p.m.

Sunday, July 28

- **Breakfast** starts at 5:00 a.m. and continues until 8:00 a.m.
- **Lunch** starts after the Papal Mass, approximately 12:30 p.m., and continues until 3:00 p.m.

Picking Up Your Meals

Your registration package includes meal tickets that are colour coded to help you identify the locations to obtain your meals. Internationally recognized symbols, accompanied by text in English, French, Spanish, and Italian, indicate food service locations.

You will be fed in groups of six, with one person picking up the entire meal for all six people.

Special Dietary Needs

Vegetarians: A vegetarian option is offered at each meal at all pavilions.

Allergies: All menus are prepared with minimal use of the most common food allergens, although trace amounts may be present. To address allergy concerns, any food items that contain nuts are clearly identified on the packaging labels.

A full list of ingredients is available at each food pavilion. People with food allergies should speak to the pavilion managers.

Other Food Services

At both Exhibition Place and Downsview Lands, concessions offer a variety of foods from many cultures. Bring some money with you if you would like to try some of the delicious food and beverage items available.

Water

With each meal you receive a 500-mL bottle of water. You can refill your water bottle, at no charge, at refill stations in Exhibition Place, along the Pilgrimage routes, and at Downsview Lands. You should drink water throughout the day and take every opportunity to refill your water bottle. You can buy water and other cold drinks at Exhibition Place and Downsview Lands, and throughout the city.

SCHEDULE OF EVENTS

The program provides you with the opportunity to have an experience of the Church through meetings with the Pope, the pastors of the Church and other pilgrims.

The major gatherings of all participants are:

- **Opening Mass of Welcome** on Tuesday, July 23 at 5:00 p.m., at Exhibition Place

- **Papal Welcoming Ceremony** on Thursday, July 25 at 5:00 p.m., at Exhibition Place

- **Way of the Cross** on Friday, July 26 at 7:30 p.m., along University Avenue

- **Vigil with the Pope** on Saturday, July 27 at 7:30 p.m., at Downsview Lands

- **Papal Mass** on Sunday, July 28 at 9:30 a.m., at Downsview Lands

---

Monday, July 22

Arrival in Toronto

You arrive in the Greater Toronto Area, settle into your accommodation and meet the young people who — along with local churches and the entire community — will be your hosts.

Tuesday, July 23

Opening Mass of Welcome
Afternoon/Evening

- His Eminence Aloysius Cardinal Ambrozic, Archbishop of Toronto, celebrates the Eucharist at Exhibition Place at 5:00 p.m.

- Opening Concert featuring Canadian talent at Exhibition Place

- Sacrament of Reconciliation

Wednesday, July 24

Morning
- Catecheses (times of prayer, discussion and reflection based on the teachings of bishops from around the world)
- A Mass concludes the catecheses.

Afternoon and Evening
- Social Service
- Youth Festival consisting of spiritual, cultural and entertainment activities
- Sacrament of Reconciliation

Thursday, July 25

Papal Welcoming Ceremony
Morning
- Catecheses (see Wednesday)

Afternoon
- Papal Welcoming Ceremony at Exhibition Place at 5:00 p.m
- Sacrament of Reconciliation

Evening
- Youth Festival
- Sacrament of Reconciliation

Friday, July 26

Way of the Cross
Morning
- Catecheses (as on previous days)

Afternoon
- Social Service
- Youth Festival
- STREETFEST!
- Sacrament of Reconciliation

Evening
- Way of the Cross along University Avenue at 7:30 p.m.

Saturday, July 27

Morning and afternoon
- Morning Mass at 8:00 a.m. at parishes throughout Toronto
- Walking pilgrimage to Downsview Lands
- Welcome Concert at Downsview Lands
- Sacrament of Reconciliation

Vigil with the Pope
Evening
- The Vigil begins at 7:30 p.m. with prayer, music, testimonies and a message from the Pope.
- The Pope leaves after the Vigil and you sleep outside at Downsview Lands.

Sunday, July 28

Papal Mass
- From 9:30 a.m. until noon, the Pope celebrates Mass at Downsview Lands. This event is open to all members of the public.

LANGUAGES FOR SIMULTANEOUS TRANSLATION

Simultaneous translation radio broadcasts are offered at the

- Opening Mass of Welcome, July 23
- Papal Welcoming Ceremony, July 25
- Way of the Cross, July 26
- Vigil with the Pope, July 27
- Papal Mass, July 28

The information contained in this chart is subject to change.

Language	Frequency – FM band	Language	Frequency – FM band
English	104.9	French	103.9
Spanish	101.7	Italian	102.7
Portuguese	99.5	Polish	91.9
German	90.7	Arabic	98.7

YOUTH FESTIVAL

The Youth Festival brings together young people to express their traditions, cultures, languages and experience of the world. It takes place on the evenings of July 23 through July 25, and on the afternoons of July 24 and 25. Events include:

Performances

Five hundred music, dance, drama and film performances will take place at 25 stages.

STREETFEST!

Buskers perform along University Avenue during the afternoon of Friday, July 26.

Prayer

The wide variety of prayer and praise experiences will be highlighted at Toronto churches and other locations.

Exhibits

Exhibits on the themes of art, culture, vocations, social service and social justice will be held at Exhibition Place.

Seminars

Discussion forums on a wide range of subjects will be held at numerous locations.

Gatherings

Opportunities to meet and celebrate based on a common spirituality, language or ethnicity will be held at churches and parks.

Cafés

Informal discussions will take place at cafés, some of which will have Internet stations.

Vocation Activities

The Vocation and Service Pavilion at Exhibition Place offers a place where you can reflect on a potential calling from God. It will also provides the chance to meet, talk and celebrate with others.

Film Festival

A selection of films with religious themes will be shown, including the world premiere of a documentary about Mother Teresa.

Images of Salvation

The Royal Ontario Museum (ROM) is hosting *Images of Salvation*, which contains over 100 artifacts from the Vatican Museums and other Italian collections. The ROM is located at 100 Queen's Park, at Bloor Street West and Avenue Road, by the Museum subway station. The ROM's extended hours from July 21–27 are 10:00 a.m. to 9:30 p.m. You will receive a special admission rate of $5 with your WYD Pass.

Recreation

Some Toronto parks will offer activities for those who want to take part in games or sports.

Social Service

You have the chance to take part in social service activities to provide a legacy of caring and to demonstrate our faith with our brothers and sisters of all faiths. Groups which have registered for Social Service will attend a three-hour session from 2:30 to 5:30 p.m. on Wednesday, July 24 and Friday, July 26.

There are three types of Social Service activities:

- service projects that directly help people
- discussions on specific service themes
- visits to local service organizations

Catecheses

Catecheses take place on Wednesday, July 24, Thursday, July 25, and Friday, July 26, organized by language groups at many locations. Bishops from around the world lead these morning sessions about the teachings of the Catholic faith, which include participation in the sacraments of Holy Eucharist and Reconciliation.

The catecheses themes are:

Wednesday: *You Are the Salt of the Earth*
Thursday: *You Are the Light of the World*
Friday: *Be Reconciled to God*

Sacrament of Reconciliation

You will have three occasions to take advantage of the Sacrament of Reconciliation:

• Priests are available during the mornings of Wednesday, July 24 to Friday, July 26 at catechesis sites.

- At Duc in Altum Park, just east of the main gates of Exhibition Place, several hundred priests are available:
  - Tuesday, July 23 from 2:00 p.m. to 4:00 p.m. and from 6:00 p.m. to 8:00 p.m.
  - Wednesday, July 24 from 2:00 p.m. to 8:00 p.m.
  - Thursday, July 25 from 2:00 p.m. to 4:00 p.m. and from 6:00 p.m. to 8:00 p.m.
  - Friday, July 26 from 2:00 p.m. to 6:00 p.m.
- On Saturday, July 27, at Downsview Lands, priests are available from 2:00 p.m. until the start of the Vigil with the Pope.

WYD STORE

You can buy official merchandise at three locations. The WYD store is located at 433 Yonge Street, near the College subway station. Exhibition Place and Downsview Lands have large vending villages where you can buy souvenirs, books, music and clothing.

VOLUNTEERS

- Volunteers are at all events to help you and event organizers. They are also at the WYD Info Booths located throughout the city.
- Volunteers can communicate in the four official WYD languages: English, French, Spanish and Italian. Do not hesitate to ask a volunteer for help.
- Volunteers wear blue shirts bearing the logo shown below.

BÉNÉVOLE
WYD2002JMJ
VOLUNTEER

RESPECTING THE ENVIRONMENT

- Specially marked cardboard boxes are available for paper waste such as newspapers, magazines, clean food wrappers, bottles and cans. Large paper bags are available for food waste. Please follow the instructions on the boxes and bags and recycle whenever possible.

- At Downsview Lands, your help is needed to move full recycling containers to the road for collection and to take empty containers back to your area to be filled.

- Whenever possible, please pick up litter and put it in the appropriate container.

- On most major streets, containers are available for waste disposal and recycling.

TELEPHONES

- A local call from a public telephone costs 25 cents ($0.25). Canadian telephone numbers have a minimum of seven digits, with some larger cities, including Toronto and surrounding area, requiring an additional three-digit area code for local calls. The area codes for Toronto are 416 and 647; for the Greater Toronto Area the area codes are 905 and 289.

- Long-distance calls within Canada and from Canada to the United States require you to dial 1 + area code + local number. Calls to other countries are made by dialling 011 + country code + city code + local number. For person-to-person calls, Calling Card calls, third-party billing and collect calls, dial 01 + country code + city code + local number. The list of country codes is found in the front section of white pages telephone directories.

- You can buy $10 and $20 official phone cards at WYD registration sites, Downsview Lands and Exhibition Place. There are 12 cards in this collectible series. You can use them for worldwide calls from Canada and the USA.

- You can also rent cellular phones at many locations.

INTERNET ACCESS

- The 98 branches of the Toronto Public Libraries (TPL) offer free high-speed Internet access.
- The main TPL branch, Toronto Reference Library (789 Yonge Street, one block north of Bloor Street) contains over 100 computer workstations and carries over 100 newspapers from around the world.
- For more information, call TPL Answerline at (416) 393-7131.
- Internet access is also available at some Youth Festival cafés.

ELECTRICITY

Canada is on the 110 volt system, unlike Europe and many countries around the world, which use the 220–240 volt system.

MONEY AND TAXES

- Canadian currency uses dollars and cents. The American dollar offers a favourable exchange rate.
- To receive the best exchange rate, change your money at a recognized financial institution, such as a bank, trust company or currency exchange.
- Canada's one- and two-dollar coins are often referred to as the *loonie* and the *toonie*. Each denomination of paper money has its own colour and design. Many businesses do not accept bills of a value of $50 or greater.

Canadian Sales Taxes

The Goods and Services Tax (GST) is a 7 percent federal tax that applies to most goods and services. Toronto, as part of the province of Ontario, also has a Provincial Sales Tax (PST) of 8 percent that will be applied to most goods you buy.

Visitor Tax Rebates

- Non-resident visitors to Canada are entitled to a GST rebate on certain goods they take out of Canada, as well as on short-term accommodations.

- Keep receipts of your purchases and accommodations if you wish to apply for a GST rebate. You can pick up a copy of the Tax Refund Application for Visitors at any Canada Customs office or at most tourism information centres, duty-free shops, department stores and some hotels.

- Visitor Tax Rebate Refunds are also available at many booths at Downsview Lands and Exhibition Place. Bring your purchase receipts and identification that shows you do not live in Canada for your rebate to be processed quickly.

Credit Cards / Bank Machines

- Major credit cards such as Visa, MasterCard, American Express and Diners Club are widely accepted. Your financial institution will automatically convert Canadian dollars into your country's currency in your monthly statement.

- Most Canadian automated banking machines (ABMs) accept your bank card on the Interac, Cirrus and Plus systems. In addition to banks, you will find ABMs in airports, some government buildings and many stores.

- If you lose your bank or credit card, immediately contact your financial institution and report the loss to police.

POSTAL SERVICES

- If you want to buy stamps, they are on sale at many pharmacies, variety and convenience stores, in addition to official Canada Post outlets.

- You can mail letters or postcards by depositing them in Canada Post mailboxes, which are found at or near most major intersections.

- If you need other postal services, such as sending a package or a registered letter, you will need to find a Canada Post outlet. These are found in designated commercial businesses, such as pharmacies, business supply stores, and other stores. Stores containing a Canada Post outlet display the Canada Post logo(shown below) on their signs or in their windows.
- Standard letter rates, including postcards, are: $0.48 in Canada; $0.65 to the United States; and $1.25 to all other countries.

CANADA POSTES
POST CANADA

From anywhere... De partout...
to anyone jusqu'à vous

FRANÇAIS

TABLE DES MATIÈRES

SYMBOLES

Ordures/Recyclage

Hôpital pour pèlerins Premiers soins

Hôpital de région/ville

Sécurité

Inscription

Eau potable

Eau non potable

Cafétéria pour les pèlerins

Toilette

Information

Service restauration

Toilette Messieurs

Autobus/ Arrêt d'autobus

TAXI

Lieu de rencontre des personnes aux besoins spéciaux

Toilette Dames

Estrade

Accessible en fauteuil roulant

Magasins

Risque d'électrocution

Danger

Accessible en fauteuil roulant avec assistance

Objets trouvés

Faites attention

Aire de visionnement pour personnes aux besoins spéciaux

Téléphone

BÉNÉVOLE WYD2002JMJ VOLUNTEER

Transport en commun

Toilette accessible en fauteuil roulant

Lieu de rencontre Pèlerins perdus

Toronto Transit Commission

Aire de repos pour personnes aux besoins spéciaux

Internet

Transit

GO Transit

SANTÉ

Si vous avez besoin d'assistance médicale

En cas d'urgence médicale, composez le 911 en tout temps et en tout lieu.

Vous pouvez composer ce numéro gratuitement à partir de n'importe quel poste téléphonique. Informez l'opérateur des Services d'urgence que vous êtes un participant de la JMJ et indiquez l'endroit où vous êtes. L'opérateur vous aidera en vous donnant les instructions pertinentes.

Si vous êtes sur les lieux où se déroulent les événements de la JMJ

- Prévenez tout bénévole ou travailleur paramédical de la JMJ. Les bénévoles qui portent une chemise rouge marquée d'une croix blanche sont des travailleurs de la santé qualifiés.
- Rendez-vous à l'unité de soins de santé de la JMJ la plus proche, que vous reconnaîtrez par une croix blanche à l'intérieur d'un cercle rouge.

Partout à Toronto

Communiquez vos besoins à votre dirigeant de groupe ou à votre hôte et ils vous dirigeront vers le centre médical le plus proche.

- Faites-vous toujours accompagner lorsque vous allez vous faire soigner.
- Lorsque vous allez dans une clinique ou à l'hôpital, informez le personnel médical que vous êtes un participant de la JMJ.
- Ayez toujours sur vous votre numéro d'assurance. Conservez vos reçus médicaux.

Pour se protéger du soleil et de la chaleur

L'été à Toronto peut être extrêmement chaud et humide. Voici quelques conseils pour vous protéger du soleil et de la chaleur :

- Portez un chapeau et abritez-vous à l'ombre. Vous pouvez

encore vous protéger du soleil en utilisant une ombrelle.

- Portez des vêtements qui protègent votre peau autant que possible.
- Portez des lunettes de soleil qui protègent contre les rayons ultraviolets A et B.
- Utilisez des crèmes solaires offrant un facteur de protection solaire (FPS) d'au moins 15. Appliquez de nouveau toutes les deux ou trois heures.
- Les températures peuvent varier considérablement au cours d'une journée. Portez plusieurs épaisseurs de vêtements afin de pouvoir vous adapter à ces changements.
- Buvez beaucoup d'eau et ayez une bouteille d'eau avec vous en tout temps.
- L'eau du robinet à Toronto est potable. Vous pouvez aussi vous procurer de l'eau embouteillée très facilement.

Lois en vigueur à Toronto sur la consommation du tabac et des boissons alcoolisées

- À Toronto et dans tout l'Ontario, l'âge légal pour boire est de 19 ans. La consommation d'alcool est interdite en dehors des bars et des restaurants, sauf sur les terrasses extérieures désignées à cet effet.
- Pour acheter des cigarettes ou autres produits du tabac, vous devez être âgé d'au moins 19 ans.
- Il est interdit de fumer tant à l'intérieur que dans la cour des écoles ou à l'intérieur de la plupart des édifices publics. Avant d'allumer une cigarette dans un lieu public, renseignez-vous pour savoir si c'est une zone où il est permis de fumer.
- Bon nombre de restaurants à Toronto sont sans-fumée; seuls les restaurants dotés d'une salle totalement fermée désignée pour fumeurs permettent l'usage du tabac. On peut fumer dans les bars sauf indication contraire. Les restaurants qui permettent de fumer dans des salles non fermées ne peuvent recevoir des clients de moins de 19 ans.

Autres conseils sur la santé

- Le service de santé publique de la ville de Toronto lance parfois des alertes au smog en cas de mauvaise qualité de l'air. Si vous souffrez d'asthme, d'allergies ou de problèmes cardiaques ou pulmonaires, vous devez éviter tout surmenage. Réduisez vos activités, restez au frais et buvez beaucoup d'eau. Si vous ne vous sentez pas bien, faites-vous soigner.

- Toutes les plages de Toronto ont des panneaux indiquant si on peut s'y baigner en toute sécurité. Certains lieux de baignade ne sont pas surveillés. Faites-vous toujours accompagner par un ami lorsque vous vous baignez, et suivez les règlements affichés.

- Si vous avez été mordu ou griffé par un animal, informez-en le dirigeant de votre groupe, votre hôte, un membre du personnel de la JMJ ou un bénévole. Lavez la blessure avec du savon et de l'eau chaude et nettoyez-la à fond. Faites-vous soigner.

PÈLERINS AUX BESOINS SPÉCIAUX

Les événements, les cérémonies et les célébrations de la JMJ ont été planifiés et organisés pour que des personnes aux besoins spéciaux puissent y participer lorsque possible. Des symboles acceptés internationalement seront également affichés sur les lieux où se déroulent les événements pour assister et orienter les personnes aux besoins spéciaux.

Transport des personnes aux besoins spéciaux

La JMJ a fait tout en son pouvoir pour assurer le transport des pèlerins à mobilité réduite aux événements. Mais ces derniers sont responsables de leur transport pour les sorties non organisées par la JMJ. Voici quelques compagnies offrant un service de transport adapté : Wheel-Trans 416 393-4222; Royal Taxi Services 416 955-0564; Beck Taxi 416 751-5555; TPT 416 209-0950; et Able Atlantic Taxi 416 291-4363.

POUR UN SÉJOUR EN TOUTE SÉCURITÉ

Toronto est l'une des villes les plus sécuritaires du monde, mais les voyageurs devraient toujours faire preuve de prudence dans un environnement non familier.

Sécurité personnelle

- Lorsque c'est possible, voyagez en groupe et utilisez le système de surveillance mutuelle.
- Marchez d'un pas assuré et soyez toujours conscients de ce qui se passe autour de vous.
- Marchez dans des zones bien éclairées, de préférence du côté de la rue où se trouvent les lampadaires.
- Après la tombée de la nuit, évitez les raccourcis traversant des terrains vagues, des ruelles, des parcs ou des cours d'école.
- Si vous avez l'impression qu'on vous suit, rendez-vous au lieu public le plus proche et appelez la police en composant le 911.
- Dans les bars ou les clubs de danse, ne laissez *jamais* votre verre sans surveillance et n'acceptez jamais de comprimé de qui que ce soit.

Pour garder vos effets en toute sécurité

- Personnalisez votre sac à dos JMJ et tout autre sac que vous avez avec des choses que vous pouvez facilement reconnaître. Il peut s'agir du drapeau de votre pays, d'un écusson ou d'un morceau de tissu coloré.
- Placez des étiquettes porte-adresse à l'intérieur et à l'extérieur de votre sac à dos et de tout autre sac que vous avez. Inscrivez seulement votre nom et votre pays d'origine sur les étiquettes; n'inscrivez aucun renseignement personnel. Utilisez des cadenas à bagages pour verrouiller les petits compartiments à glissière.
- Placez des insignes porte-nom sur vos vêtements.
- Gardez les médicaments de prescription avec vous en tout temps.

- N'apportez pas de grosses sommes d'argent avec vous; utilisez des chèques de voyage ou des cartes de crédit lorsque possible. Un petit sac à porter à la taille est plus sûr qu'une sacoche ou un portefeuille.
- Ne laissez jamais vos effets sans surveillance, surtout dans les aéroports ou les gares routières et ferroviaires.
- Lorsque possible, laissez vos documents de voyage et tout objet de valeur en lieu sûr là où vous séjournez. Ne les apportez pas avec vous sur les lieux où se déroulent les événements.
- Photocopiez tout document de voyage important tel passe-port, billet d'avion, etc. Notez quelque part les numéros de série de vos chèques de voyage et de tout équipement électronique que vous avez, ainsi que les numéros de compte de vos cartes de crédit. Signalez immédiatement tout document de voyage ou personnel perdu ou volé à la police ou à un bénévole qui pourra vous diriger vers l'agent de police le plus proche.

Sécurité-incendie

Précautions :

- Les flammes nues, y compris les chandelles allumées, sont interdites partout sur les lieux d'hébergement.
- Gardez les chandelles allumées loin des matières inflammables et ne laissez jamais une chandelle allumée sans surveillance.
- Composez le 416 338-9050 pour signaler tout risque d'incendie.

Si vous découvrez un incendie dans un immeuble :

- Quittez la zone immédiatement et aidez toute personne en danger à quitter les lieux.
- Activez l'avertisseur d'incendie et alertez le personnel.
- Suivez les instructions données sur la liste qui suit.

Si vous entendez une alarme d' incendie dans un immeuble :

- Suivez les instructions données par le personnel de l'immeuble.
- Quittez l'immeuble immédiatement.
- Fermez toutes les portes derrière vous.
- Utilisez les escaliers pour quitter l'immeuble, n'utilisez pas les ascenseurs.
- Dirigez-vous vers la zone désignée pour le rassemblement à l'extérieur de l'immeuble. Ne retournez pas dans l'immeuble.

PASSEPORT OU VISA PERDU OU VOLÉ

Si votre passeport est perdu ou volé, vous devez signaler cet incident au poste de police le plus proche. Vous devriez aussi entrer en contact avec le consulat ou l'ambassade de votre pays pour signaler l'incident et en obtenir un autre. La liste d'ambassades et de consulats apparaissant au dos de ce guide contient les renseignements dont vous aurez besoin pour communiquer avec les dignitaires de votre pays.

OBJETS TROUVÉS

Les services policiers de Toronto mettront en place des bureaux des objets trouvés à Exhibition Place et sur les terrains de Downsview où vous pourrez signaler la perte d'un objet perdu ou remettre un objet que vous avez trouvé.

VOTRE SAC À DOS

Dans votre sac à dos vous trouverez les objets suivants :

– carte de Toronto
– épinglette JMJ
– foulard JMJ
– chandelles
– porte-chandelle
– croix
– chapelet
– épinglette du Canada
– drapeau canadien
– étiquettes porte-adresse
– cartes postales

Remarque : lorsque vous recevrez votre sac à dos, on vous remettra également le livre de liturgie, le guide du pèlerin et votre laissez-passer.

VOTRE LAISSEZ-PASSER

• Votre laissez-passer vous permettra de participer à tous les événements de la JMJ. Il vous permettra également d'utiliser le réseau de transport public de Toronto sans coût durant la JMJ.

• Veuillez remplir votre laissez-passer en y inscrivant les importants détails demandés. Vous trouverez les numéros de secours et d'information de la JMJ sur le laissez-passer.

• Contribuez au succès de la JMJ en portant votre laissez-passer bien en vue en tout temps.

• La bordure colorée de votre laissez-passer correspond à la couleur de la section qui vous a été attribuée à Downsview.

• Si vous perdez votre laissez-passer, rendez-vous au kiosque Info ou au centre d'inscription de la JMJ pour obtenir de l'aide.

COMPORTEMENT ACCEPTABLE

Lors de votre séjour à Toronto, votre comportement a des répercussions sur tous les jeunes catholiques. Vous serez expulsé si vous affichez un comportement offensant qui perturbe le déroulement des activités officielles.

HÉBERGEMENT

Des équipes qualifiées seront présentes dans tous les lieux d'hébergement de la JMJ pour vous aider. Ces bénévoles sont vos hôtes. Suivez toutes les instructions relatives à la sécurité et portez à leur attention tout problème et toute inquiétude que vous avez.

Hébergement de groupes dans les écoles et ailleurs

• Vous devrez toujours présenter votre laissez-passer pour accéder aux lieux d'hébergement.

• Respectez les heures d'arrivée et de départ données par les équipes hôtes. Les lieux d'hébergement de la JMJ sont ouverts pour vous de 20 h à 9 h. Les locaux sont verrouillés à toute autre heure de la journée et personne n'y sera admis. Si vous tombez malade et que vous n'êtes pas capable de participer aux activités de la journée, on vous dirigera vers l'infirmerie de la JMJ la plus proche.

• Utilisez uniquement les aires publiques et évitez le plus que possible de faire du bruit dans les dortoirs. Évitez tout comportement perturbateur et respectez le droit des autres pèlerins à la vie privée et au calme.

• La consommation de tabac et de boissons alcoolisées est strictement interdite sur les lieux d'hébergement de la JMJ. Si vous violez ces règlements, vous serez expulsé des lieux immédiatement et vous devrez vous arranger pour trouver un autre logement à vos frais.

• L'usage d'appareils ou d'équipement électriques (ex. : bouilloires, appareils de chauffage, etc.) est interdit.

- Les locaux sont verrouillés à 1 h. Tâchez de rentrer avant cette heure.
- Tout aliment doit être consommé à l'extérieur des propriétés. Il est interdit de prendre des repas à l'intérieur des locaux.

Familles d'accueil

- Séjourner dans une famille d'accueil est un privilège. Respectez les gens qui vous accueillent dans leur foyer.
- Il est important d'obéir aux règlements de la maison de votre hôte et à toute exigence quant aux heures de rentrée et de départ.

CIRCULER À TORONTO

Toronto est une ville facile à visiter, et la plupart des Torontois seront heureux de vous guider. N'hésitez pas à demander de l'aide si vous êtes perdu ou désorienté.

Transport public

- La Commission des transports en commun de Toronto (TTC) gère le service de transport par autobus, tramway et métro dans toute la ville. Le réseau GO gère le service d'autobus et le service ferroviaire dans la Région du Grand Toronto (RGT). Le service du transport en commun urbain est également disponible dans les régions périphériques de la RGT.
  - Pour des renseignements sur les services de la TTC, composez le 416 393-4636
  - Pour des renseignements sur les services du réseau GO, composez le 416 869-3200
- Votre inscription vous permet d'utiliser gratuitement les services de transport en commun de la TTC pour les dates inscrites sur votre inscription. En dehors de ces dates, les tarifs de base s'appliquent.
- Lorsque vous voyagez en métro, en autobus ou en tramway, n'oubliez pas les mesures de *précaution suivantes* :

– Dans les autobus, l'option « Request Stop » permet aux femmes voyageant seules entre 21 h et 5 h de demander au conducteur de les laisser descendre entre les arrêts.

– Avant de descendre d'un tramway, regardez à droite. Assurez-vous que la voie est libre.

– Des zones d'attente sont aménagées sur tous les quais de métro/réseau express. Ces zones sont bien éclairées et sont dotées d'intercom qui permet de communiquer avec le personnel de la station TTC.

– Tous les véhicules de métro/réseau express sont dotés de système d'alarme pour l'assistance aux passagers. Activez cette alarme pour signaler tout incendie, acte de harcèlement, maladie, acte de vandalisme ou tout incident qui porte atteinte à la sécurité des passagers.

Taxis

• Au centre-ville de Toronto, on peut facilement prendre un taxi dans les rues. Une lumière allumée sur le toit d'un taxi signifie qu'il est disponible. Pour appeler un taxi, consultez les Pages jaunes de l'annuaire téléphonique sous la rubrique *Taxis*.

• Veillez à ce que le compteur soit activé avant de commencer le trajet. Payez le montant indiqué par le compteur. Le pourboire est facultatif.

• Bien que le service de taxis soit disponible partout à Toronto, il peut être très coûteux. Le tarif à payer pour un trajet du centre-ville à la grande banlieue peut être très élevé. Il est possible de demander au répartiteur d'une compagnie de taxi ou à un chauffeur de vous donner un tarif approximatif avant de décider d'entreprendre un trajet.

• À Toronto, tant les chauffeurs que les véhicules de taxi doivent être titulaires d'un permis. La photo du chauffeur et les informations concernant le propriétaire du taxi doivent être affichées dans le taxi à l'arrière de l'appui-tête. Pour porter plainte ou obtenir des renseignements, composez le 1-877-868-2947.

Stationner dans les rues de Toronto ou sur une propriété privée

• Les règlements sur le stationnement sont *strictement* appliqués aussi bien par la police que les agents de stationnement, et les contraventions sont coûteuses. Pour éviter qu'on remorque votre véhicule, observez les instructions données sur les panneaux de signalisation et ne laissez votre véhicule sur aucune propriété sauf s'il s'agit d'une aire désignée pour le stationnement.

• Si vous stationnez dans un parc de stationnement sans personnel, suivez les règlements qui y sont affichés.

• Pour obtenir des renseignements ou porter plainte au sujet du stationnement, composez le 416 392-3082.

Conduire à Toronto

• Pour obtenir des renseignements routiers, composez le 416 599-9090.

• Aucun véhicule ne pourra accéder à Exhibition Place ni à Downsview durant la JMJ.

LIEUX OÙ SE DÉROULENT LES ÉVÉNEMENTS

Les appareils radio émetteurs-récepteurs et les talkie-walkie sont interdits sur tous les sites et seront désactivés une fois qu'ils seront détectés. Veuillez utiliser des téléphones cellulaires pour communiquer.

Exhibition Place

Situé près du centre-ville de Toronto, juste au nord du lac Ontario, Exhibition Place sera ouvert de 9 h à 22 h du lundi 22 juillet au jeudi 25 juillet, et de 9 h à 18 h le vendredi 26 juillet.

Exhibition Place est l'un des lieux où se tiendront les catéchèses du mercredi 24 juillet au vendredi 26 juillet. En après-midi, le parc Duc in Altum situé tout près est disponible pour le Sacrement de la réconciliation. En après-midi et en soirée, Exhibition Place accueillera le Festival de la jeunesse.

Tous les participants se rendront à Exhibition Place pour la **Cérémonie d'accueil du Pape** à 17 h le jeudi 25 juillet.

Objets et activités interdits à Exhibition Place :

- propane
- barbecues
- camping
- patins à roues alignées
- bicyclettes
- trottinettes
- planches à roulettes
- bouteilles en verre
- boissons alcoolisées
- feux d'artifice

Tout ce que vous avez en votre possession peut faire l'objet d'une fouille.

Avenue University

L'avenue University est l'une des principales artères de Toronto. Dès 19 h 30 le vendredi 26 juillet, la cérémonie du **Chemin de Croix** commencera à Nathan Phillips Square, devant l'hôtel de ville de Toronto. La procession se poursuivra vers le nord sur l'avenue University, passera devant l'Assemblée législative de l'Ontario et l'Université de Toronto, et prendra fin au Musée royal de l'Ontario près de la rue Bloor.

Terrains de Downsview

Les pèlerins convergeront vers les terrains de Downsview au nord-ouest de Toronto, à 15 km de Exhibition Place, le samedi 27 juillet. Il convient de noter qu'on ne vous permettra pas d'accéder à Downsview avant 8 h le samedi 27 juillet. On vous indiquera l'un des quatre trajets pour vous y rendre, chacun correspondant à une marche d'environ 8 km.

Vous participerez à une **Vigile avec le Pape**, qui comprendra des prières, des chants, des lectures bibliques, des témoignages et un message du Pape à compter de 19 h 30 le 27 juillet. Suite à la vigile, le Pape se retirera pour la nuit alors que vous dormirez à la belle étoile sur les terrains de Downsview.

Le dimanche 28 juillet, le Pape célébrera une messe à 9 h 30 pour clôturer la JMJ. La messe est ouverte aux membres du public. Restez sur les lieux pendant au moins une heure après la **messe papale**, afin de permettre au public de partir les premiers. La JMJ vous demande également de nettoyer les lieux en ramassant les déchets sauvages que vous placerez dans les poubelles ou sacs à ordures prévus à cet effet. Vous *devez* quitter les lieux au plus tard à 21 h le 28 juillet.

Il convient de noter que tous les objets et activités interdits à Exhibition Place le sont également à Downsview, à l'exception du camping dans la nuit du samedi 27 juillet.

REPAS

Plan de repas complet

Ce plan comprend 11 repas, du repas du soir le mardi 23 juillet au repas du midi le dimanche 28 juillet.

Plan de repas de fin de semaine

Le plan de repas de fin de semaine comprend trois repas : repas du soir le samedi 27 juillet, petit déjeuner et repas du midi le dimanche 28 juillet.

Les menus

Dans les menus on trouve une grande variété de mets de diverses cultures. Huit des 11 repas offerts dans le plan de repas complet comprennent un plat principal chaud. Les repas froids en boîte sont fournis de sorte que vous puissiez participer aux événements qui se déroulent à divers endroits dans la ville sans devoir retourner à votre buffet.

Le menu a été préparé en s'inspirant du Guide alimentaire canadien pour manger sainement, et satisfait aux exigences des programmes nutritionnels.

Un plat végétarien est offert à chaque repas.

Heures et lieux des repas

Les repas seront servis dans des pavillons situés à Exhibition Place et à Downsview. L'attribution de buffet est effectuée en fonction des lieux de catéchèse.

Mardi 23 juillet

- **Le repas du soir** sera servi après la messe d'ouverture vers 18 h 30 et jusqu'à 22 h.

Mercredi 24 juillet

- **Le repas du midi** sera servi après les catéchèses, aux environs de midi trente jusqu'à 14 h 30.
- **Le repas du soir** sera servi de 17 h 30 à 20 h.

Jeudi 25 juillet

- **Le repas du midi** sera servi après les catéchèses aux environs de midi trente et jusqu'à 14 h 30.
- Tous les participants recevront **un repas du soir** à Exhibition Place après la cérémonie d'accueil du Pape, de 18 h 30 jusqu'à 22 h.

Vendredi 26 juillet

- **Le repas du midi** sera servi après les catéchèses aux environs de midi trente et jusqu'à 14 h 30.
- De 12 h 30 à 14 h 30, à votre buffet, vous pourrez également vous procurer une **boîte-repas** pour votre repas du soir, afin que tous puissent participer au Chemin de croix.

Samedi 27 juillet

- Un **repas en boîte** sera distribué aux pèlerins entre 8 h 30 et 16 h sur le parcours de pèlerinage qui leur a été attribué.

Service alimentaire à Downsview

Le plan de repas de Downsview de même que le plan de repas de fin de semaine comprennent les trois repas suivants :

Samedi 27 juillet

- **Le repas du soir** sera servi de 16 h à 19 h.

Dimanche 28 juillet

- **Le petit déjeuner** sera servi de 5 h à 8 h.
- **Le repas du midi** sera servi après la messe papale, aux environs de midi trente jusqu'à 15 h.

Pour obtenir vos repas

Votre trousse d'inscription comprend des bons de repas à couleur indicative pour vous permettre d'identifier les lieux où obtenir vos repas. Des symboles acceptés internationalement accompagnés de textes en anglais, français, espagnol et italien indiquent les endroits où sont situés les services alimentaires.

Vous serez servis par groupe de six pèlerins, alors que les repas pour tout le groupe seront remis à une seule personne.

Besoins alimentaires particuliers

Végétariens : Une option végétarienne sera offerte à chaque repas dans chaque pavillon.

Allergies : tous les repas sont préparés en utilisant le moins possible les allergènes alimentaires les plus communs, bien qu'il soit possible qu'on y trouve des teneurs négligeables. Pour éviter les problèmes d'allergies, tout produit alimentaire qui contient des noix sera clairement identifié sur les étiquettes d'emballage.

Une liste complète des ingrédients sera disponible dans chaque pavillon alimentaire. Les personnes qui sont allergiques à certains aliments devraient en parler aux responsables.

Autres services alimentaires

Tant à Exhibition Place qu'à Downsview, des traiteurs offriront une grande variété de mets de diverses cultures. Apportez de l'argent avec vous au cas où cela vous tente d'essayer quelques-uns des mets et boissons délicieux qui seront disponibles.

Eau

Avec chaque repas vous recevrez une bouteille d'eau de 500 ml. Vous pouvez remplir votre bouteille gratuitement dans les endroits désignés à cet effet à Exhibition Place, le long des routes de pèlerinage et sur les terrains de Downsview. Vous devrez boire de l'eau durant toute la journée et profiter de toute occasion qui se présente pour remplir votre bouteille. Vous pourrez acheter de l'eau et autres boissons froides à Exhibition Place et Downsview, et partout dans la ville.

HORAIRE DES ÉVÉNEMENTS

Le programme vous offre l'occasion de vivre une expérience d'Église à travers les rencontres avec le Pape, les pasteurs de l'Église et les autres pèlerins.

Principaux événements rassemblant tous les participants :

- **Messe d'ouverture,** le mardi 23 juillet, à 17 h, à Exhibition Place

- **Cérémonie d'accueil du Pape,** le jeudi 25 juillet, à 17 h, à Exhibition Place

- **Chemin de croix,** le vendredi 26 juillet, à 19 h 30, le long de l'avenue University

- **Vigile avec le Pape,** le samedi 27 juillet, à 19 h 30, sur les terrains de Downsview

- **Messe papale,** le dimanche 28 juillet, à 9 h 30, sur les terrains de Downsview

Lundi 22 juillet

Arrivée à Toronto

Vous arrivez dans la Région du Grand Toronto où vous allez vous installer dans votre lieu d'hébergement et rencontrer les jeunes qui — avec les églises locales et la communauté entière — vous accueilleront.

Mardi 23 juillet

Messe d'ouverture

Après-midi/soirée

- Son Éminence le Cardinal Aloysius Ambrozic, archevêque de Toronto, préside l'Eucharistie à Exhibition Place, à 17 h.
- Concert d'ouverture mettant en vedette des artistes canadiens à Exhibition Place.
- Sacrement de la réconciliation

Mercredi 24 juillet

Matinée

- Catéchèses (périodes de prière, de discussion et de réflexion sur les enseignements des évêques du monde entier).
- Messe clôturant les catéchèses.

Après-midi/soirée

- Services à caractère social
- Festival de la jeunesse (activités spirituelles, culturelles et distractives)
- Sacrement de la réconciliation

Jeudi 25 juillet

Cérémonie d'accueil du Pape

Matin

- Catéchèses (voir mercredi)

Après-midi

- Cérémonie d'accueil du Pape à Exhibition Place, à 17 h
- Sacrement de la réconciliation

Soir

- Festival de la jeunesse
- Sacrement de la réconciliation

Vendredi 26 juillet

Chemin de croix

Matin

- Catéchèses (comme durant les jours précédents)

Après-midi

- Services à caractère social
- Festival de la jeunesse
- STREETFEST!
- Sacrement de la réconciliation

Soir

- Chemin de croix le long de l'avenue University, à 19 h 30

Samedi 27 juillet

Matin et après-midi

- Messe matinale, à 8 h, dans des paroisses de Toronto
- Pèlerinage à Downsview
- Concert d'accueil à Downsview
- Sacrement de la réconciliation

Vigile avec le Pape
Soir

- La vigile commence à 19 h 30 avec des prières, de la musique, des témoignages et un message du Pape.
- Le Pape part après la vigile alors que vous dormirez à la belle étoile sur les terrains de Downsview.

Dimanche 28 juillet

Messe papale

- De 9 h 30 jusqu'à midi, le Pape préside la messe sur les terrains de Downsview. Cet événement est ouvert au grand public.

LANGUES POUR LA TRADUCTION SIMULTANÉE

Des traductions simultanées seront radiodiffusées lors des événements suivants :

- Messe d'ouverture du 23 juillet
- Cérémonie d'accueil du Pape du 25 juillet
- Chemin de croix du 26 juillet
- Vigile avec le Pape du 27 juillet
- Messe papale du 28 juillet

Les informations présentées dans ce tableau sont sujettes à changement.

Langue	Fréquence – bande FM	Langue	Fréquence – bande FM
Anglais	104.9	Français	103.9
Espagnol	101.7	Italien	102.7
Portugais	99.5	Polonais	91.9
Allemand	90.7	Arabe	98.7

FESTIVAL DE LA JEUNESSE

Le Festival de la jeunesse rassemble les jeunes de sorte qu'ils aient l'occasion d'exprimer leurs traditions, leur culture, leur langue et leur expérience du monde. Cet événement aura lieu en soirée les 23, 24 et 25 juillet et en après-midi les 24 et 25 juillet.

Activités prévues :

Spectacles

Cinq cents représentations de diverses expressions artistiques (musique, danse, théâtre et cinéma) seront présentées sur 25 scènes.

STREETFEST!

Des amuseurs de rue se produiront le long de l'avenue University dans l'après-midi du vendredi 26 juillet.

Prières

Les églises de Toronto et autres lieux seront le théâtre de diverses manifestations de prière et de louange.

Expositions

Des expositions sur les thèmes de l'art, de la culture, des vocations, du service à caractère social et de la justice sociale seront présentées à Exhibition Place.

Séminaires

Des forums de discussion sur une grande variété de sujets seront tenus à divers endroits.

Rassemblements

Divers événements offrant des occasions de rassemblement et de célébration dans une même tradition spirituelle ou une même langue ou ethnie auront lieu dans des églises et des parcs.

Cafés

Des discussions informelles auront lieu dans des cafés dont certains seront dotés de stations Internet.

Activités vocationnelles

Le pavillon des vocations et services à Exhibition Place offre un coin tout indiqué pour réfléchir à l'appel de Dieu. Les pèlerins y trouveront également l'occasion de rencontrer d'autres personnes, d'échanger et de célébrer avec elles.

Festival du film

Une sélection de films sur des thèmes religieux seront présentés, notamment un documentaire en primeur mondiale sur Soeur Teresa.

Images du salut

Le Musée royal de l'Ontario présente une exposition *Images du salut*, qui contient plus d'une centaine de pièces provenant des musées du Vatican et autres collections italiennes. Le Musée royal de l'Ontario est situé au 100 Queen's Park, à l'intersection de la rue Bloor Ouest et de l'avenue Road, près de la station de métro Museum. Le Musée prolonge ses heures d'ouverture du 21 au 27 juillet. Il sera donc ouvert de 10 h à 21 h 30. Vous bénéficierez d'un tarif d'admission spécial de 5 $ avec votre laissez-passer de la JMJ.

Loisirs

Certains parcs de Toronto offriront des activités pour ceux et celles qui veulent participer à des jeux ou des sports.

Service à caractère social

Nous aurons l'occasion de participer à des activités de service à caractère social, de manifester notre compassion et de vivre notre foi avec nos frères et soeurs de toutes les confessions. Les groupes qui se sont inscrits pour participer aux services à caractère social auront une rencontre de trois heures, soit de 14 h 30 à 17 h 30, le mercredi 24 juillet et le vendredi 26 juillet.

Il existe trois types d'activités à caractère social :

- Projets de service qui assurent une aide directe aux gens
- Discussions sur certains sujets liés au thème service
- Visite d'organisations de service locales

Catéchèses

Organisées par groupe linguistique, les catéchèses auront lieu à divers endroits le mercredi 24 juillet, le jeudi 25 juillet et le vendredi 26 juillet. Des évêques venant de tous les coins du monde présideront ces séances matinales portant sur la foi catholique et comprenant la célébration des sacrements de l'Eucharistie et de la Réconciliation.

Thèmes des catéchèses :

Mercredi : *Vous êtes le sel de la terre*

Jeudi : *Vous êtes la lumière du monde*

Vendredi : *Soyez réconciliés avec Dieu*

Sacrement de la réconciliation

Vous aurez trois occasions de vivre le sacrement de la réconciliation :

- Des prêtres seront disponibles sur les lieux de catéchèse au cours de la matinée du mercredi 24 juillet, du jeudi 25 juillet et du vendredi 26 juillet.
- Plusieurs centaines de prêtres seront disponibles au parc Duc in Altum, juste à l'est de l'entrée principale d'Exhibition Place :
  - Mardi 23 juillet, de 14 h à 16 h et de 18 h à 20 h
  - Mercredi 24 juillet, de 14 h à 20 h
  - Jeudi 25 juillet, de 14 h à 16 h et de 18 h à 20 h
  - Vendredi 26 juillet, de 14 h à 18 h
- Le samedi 27 juillet, des prêtres seront disponibles sur les terrains de Downsview de 14 h jusqu'au début de la vigile avec le Pape.

MAGASIN DE LA JMJ

Vous pouvez acheter des produits officiels de la JMJ à trois endroits. Le magasin de la JMJ est situé au 433, rue Yonge, près de la station de métro College. Exhibition Place et Downsview ont de grands villages où vous pouvez acheter des souvenirs, des livres, de la musique et des vêtements.

BÉNÉVOLES

- Des bénévoles seront présents dans tous les événements pour vous aider et assister les organisateurs des événements. On les trouvera aussi dans les kiosques Info situés à divers endroits dans la ville.

- Les bénévoles peuvent communiquer dans les quatre langues officielles de la JMJ qui sont : l'anglais, le français, l'espagnol et l'italien. N'hésitez pas à solliciter l'aide d'un bénévole.

- Les bénévoles portent un T-shirt bleu avec le logo ci-dessous.

BÉNÉVOLE
WYD2002JMJ
VOLUNTEER

RESPECT DE L'ENVIRONNEMENT

- Des boîtes de carton spécialement marquées seront disponibles pour jeter les déchets de papier – journaux, magazines, papiers d'emballage de nourriture, les bouteilles et les contenants. De gros sacs de papier seront disponibles pour jeter des déchets d'aliments. Veuillez suivre les instructions sur les boîtes et les sacs et recyclez lorsque possible.

- Sur les terrains de Downsview, nous vous demandons d'apporter les sacs de recyclage pleins sur le bord de la route et de rapporter un sac vide sur votre site.

- Lorsque possible, ramassez les déchets sauvages et jetez-les dans le conteneur approprié.

- Sur les principales artères, on retrouve des poubelles et des sacs de recyclage.

TÉLÉPHONES

- Un appel local à partir d'un téléphone public coûte 25 cents (0,25 $). Au Canada, les numéros de téléphone contiennent au moins sept chiffres. Certaines villes, y compris Toronto et les régions périphériques, y ajoutent un code régional de trois chiffres pour les appels locaux. Les codes régionaux de Toronto sont le 416 et le 647, le 905 et le 289 étant valides pour la Région du Grand Toronto.

- Pour effectuer un appel interurbain à l'intérieur du Canada et du Canada vers les États-Unis, il faut composer de la façon suivante : 1 + code régional + numéro local. Pour les appels outre-mer, il faut faire le 011 + code pays + code ville + numéro local. Pour les appels de personne à personne, les appels par carte d'appel, la facturation à une tierce partie et les appels à frais virés, il faut composer : 01 + code pays + code ville + numéro local. La liste des codes pays apparaît dans la première section des pages blanches de l'annuaire téléphonique.

- Des cartes d'appel officielles de 10 $ et de 20 $ seront vendues sur les lieux d'inscription à Downsview et à Exhibition Place. Vous pouvez les utiliser pour des appels internationaux à partir du Canada et des États-Unis et les collectionner. La collection complète comprend 12 cartes.

- Vous pouvez également louer des téléphones cellulaires à plusieurs endroits.

ACCÈS INTERNET

- Les 98 succursales des TPL (Toronto Public Libraries) offrent un accès Internet haute vitesse.

- La bibliothèque principale, la Toronto Reference Library (789, rue Yonge, une rue au nord de la rue Bloor), contient 100 postes de travail informatisés et reçoit plus de 100 journaux de divers pays du monde entier.

- Pour de plus amples renseignements, composez le numéro du service d'information de TPL qui est le 416 393-7131.

- Les services d'accès Internet sont également offerts dans certains cafés du Festival de la jeunesse.

ÉLECTRICITÉ

Le Canada utilise un système de 110 volts, contrairement à l'Europe et à divers pays du monde où le système utilisé est de 220–240 volts.

ARGENT ET TAXES

- La monnaie canadienne est composée de dollars et de cents. Le dollar américain offre un taux de change favorable.

- Afin de recevoir le meilleur taux de change, vous aurez intérêt à échanger votre argent dans un établissement financier reconnu comme par exemple une banque, une société de fiducie ou un bureau de change.

- Au Canada, la pièce de un dollar est généralement appelée huard. Chaque billet a une couleur et un motif particuliers. Un grand nombre d'entreprises n'acceptent motif pas les billets de 50 $ ou plus.

Taxes de vente canadiennes

La taxe sur les produits et services (TPS) est une taxe fédérale de 7 % qui s'applique à la plupart des produits et des services. Une taxe de vente provinciale (TVP) de 8 % sera également appliquée à la plupart des achats effectués à Toronto et partout dans la province.

Remboursement de taxes aux visiteurs

- Les visiteurs non résidant au Canada sont admissibles à un remboursement de la TPS pour certains produits qu'ils apportent à l'étranger ainsi que pour le logement provisoire.

- Conservez les reçus des achats effectués et des frais de logement si vous désirez vous faire rembourser la TPS. Vous pouvez vous procurer un Formulaire de remboursement de taxe aux visiteurs auprès d'un bureau de l'Agence des douanes du Canada ou dans la plupart des centres d'information touristique, des boutiques hors taxes, des grands magasins et dans certains hôtels.

- Vous pourrez également vous procurer des formulaires de remboursement de taxe aux visiteurs dans plusieurs kiosques Info à Downsview et à Exhibition Place. Apportez les reçus d'achats effectués ainsi qu'une pièce d'identité qui prouve que vous ne résidez pas au Canada, de sorte qu'on puisse traiter rapidement votre demande.

Cartes de crédit / Guichets automatiques bancaires

- Les principales cartes de crédit telles Visa, MasterCard, American Express et Diners Club sont généralement acceptées. Votre institution financière convertira automatiquement les dollars canadiens dans la devise de votre pays sur votre relevé mensuel.

- La plupart des guichets automatiques bancaires accepteront votre carte bancaire sur les réseaux Interac, Cirrus et Plus. Outre les banques, vous trouverez des guichets automatiques bancaires dans les aéroports, dans certains édifices publics et dans divers magasins.

- Si vous perdez votre carte bancaire ou votre carte de crédit, communiquez immédiatement avec votre institution bancaire et signalez l'incident à la police.

SERVICES POSTAUX

- Si vous voulez acheter des timbres, vous en trouverez dans plusieurs pharmacies et dépanneurs, en plus des points de vente officiels de la Société canadienne des postes.

- Vous pouvez poster des lettres ou des cartes postales en les déposant dans les boîtes aux lettres de la Société canadienne des postes que vous trouverez aux intersections de la plupart des grandes artères ou près de celles-ci.

- Si vous avez besoin d'autres services postaux, comme par exemple, l'envoi de colis ou de lettres recommandées, il vous faudra vous rendre dans un point de vente de la Société canadienne des postes. On les retrouve dans certains commerces comme par exemples les pharmacies, les magasins de fournitures de bureau, etc. Les magasins abritant des points de vente de la Société canadienne des postes affichent le logo de cette société (présenté ci-dessous) sur leurs enseignes ou dans leurs fenêtres.

- Le tarif postal pour une lettre ou une carte postale est de 0,48 $ au Canada; 0,65 $ aux États-Unis; et 1,25 $ pour tous les autres pays.

From anywhere...   *De partout...*
to anyone   *jusqu'à vous*

ESPAÑOL

ÍNDICE

SÍMBOLOS

 Basura/Reciclaje

 Hospital para Peregrinos Primeros Auxilios

 Hospital Regional/ Metroplitano

 Seguridad

 Inscripción

 Agua Potable

Agua No Potable

 Comida del Peregrino

 Baños

 Información

 Venta de Alimentos

 Baños para Caballeros

Autobús/ Parada de Autobús TAXI

 Lugar de Encuentro Personas con Necesidades Especiales

 Baños para Damas

Escenario

 Accesible con Silla de Ruedas

 Tiendas

Peligro Electricidad **Danger**

 Accesible con Silla de Ruedas con Ayuda

Objetos Perdidos

Atención

Área de Observación Reservada para Personas con Necesidades Especiales

 Teléfono

 Voluntarios

 Baños Accesibles con Silla de Ruedas

Lugar de Encuentro y Peregrinos Perdidos

 Toronto Transit Commission

 Área de Descanso Personas con Necesidades Especiales

 Internet

 GO Transit

SALUD

Si necesitas asistencia médica

*En caso de una emergencia médica, llama al **911** a cualquier hora y desde cualquier lugar.*

Se puede llamar a este número gratuitamente desde cualquier teléfono. Infórmale al operador de Servicios de Emergencias que eres un participante de la JMJ y dile dónde estás. El operador te ayudará dándote las instrucciones apropiadas.

En los Sitios de la JMJ

- Avisa a cualquier paramédico o voluntario de la JMJ. Los voluntarios que visten una camisa roja con una cruz blanca son asistentes sanitarios calificados.

- Dirígete a la estación sanitaria de la JMJ más cercana, marcada con una cruz blanca dentro de un círculo rojo.

Dentro de Toronto

- Avísale a tu líder de grupo o al anfitrión de tu alojamiento y ellos te indicarán el centro médico más cercano.

- Siempre que busques ayuda médica, ve con alguna otra persona.

- Cuando vayas a una clínica u hospital, dile al personal médico que eres un participante de la JMJ.

- Siempre porta el número de seguro contigo. Guarda los recibos médicos.

Precauciones con el sol y el calor

En Toronto, el verano puede ser extremadamente caluroso y húmedo. Para protegerte del sol y del calor:

- Utiliza un sombrero y busca áreas con sombra o usa una sombrilla para hacer sombra.

- Usa ropa que proteja tu piel lo máximo posible.

- Usa anteojos de sol que protejan de los rayos UVA y UVB.
- Utiliza pantalla solar con un factor de protección solar (FPS) 15 o mayor. Vuélvetelo a aplicar cada dos o tres horas.
- Vístete en capas para adaptarte a los cambios de temperatura durante el día.
- Bebe mucha agua y lleva una botella de agua contigo en todo momento.
- El agua del grifo (llave/ canilla) de Toronto es apta para el consumo. También el agua en botella se consigue con facilidad.

Leyes de Toronto que rigen el consumo de cigarrillo y de bebidas alcohólicas

- La edad permitida en Toronto, y en todo Ontario, para beber alcohol es 19 años. El consumo de alcohol no está permitido fuera de los bares y restoranes excepto en áreas externas designadas.
- Para comprar cigarrillos u otros productos de tabaco, debes tener 19 años de edad.
- No se permite fumar dentro de escuelas o en áreas escolares ni dentro de la mayoría de los edificios públicos. Antes de encender un cigarrillo en un espacio público, averigua si está permitido fumar.
- En muchos restoranes de Toronto no se puede fumar; sólo aquéllos que tienen una sala totalmente cerrada para fumadores permiten fumar. Se permite fumar en bares, a menos que se indique lo contrario. Los restoranes que permiten fumar en sectores no cerrados no pueden dejar ingresar a clientes menores de 19 años.

Otros consejos para la salud

- El departamento de salud pública de la Ciudad de Toronto puede en ocasiones mandar *alertas de smog* para indicar que la calidad del aire es pobre. Si tienes asma, alergias o algún problema cardíaco o pulmonar, tienes que tener mucho cuidado de no hacer un esfuerzo excesivo. Disminuye el ritmo de tus actividades, mantente fresco y bebe mucha agua. Si no te sientes bien, busca atención médica.

- Todas las playas de Toronto tienen señales que indican si es seguro nadar o no. Algunas áreas de nado no cuentan con alguien que supervise. Siempre nada con un amigo/ a y cumple las reglas que se indican.

- Si te muerde o te rasguña un animal, avisa al líder de tu grupo, al anfitrión del sitio donde te alojas o a un miembro del personal de la JMJ o a un voluntario de ésta. Lava la herida con jabón y agua tibia y límpiala a fondo. Busca atención médica.

PEREGRINOS CON NECESIDADES ESPECIALES

Los eventos, las ceremonias y las celebraciones de la JMJ han sido planificados y organizados para incluir a las personas con necesidades especiales siempre que sea posible. En los sitios de los eventos también hay símbolos reconocidos internacionalmente para asistir y guiar a las personas con necesidades especiales.

Transporte de los peregrinos con necesidades especiales

La JMJ ha hecho todo esfuerzo posible para asegurar que el transporte a los eventos esté disponible para los peregrinos con problemas de movilidad. Dichos peregrinos tendrán que proveer su transporte para las salidas que no sean de la JMJ. Las opciones de transporte accesible para personas con problemas de movilidad incluyen: Wheel-Trans (416) 393-4222, Royal Taxi Services (416) 955-0564, Beck Taxi (416) 751-5555, TPT (416) 209-0950 y Able Atlantic Taxi (416) 291-4363.

SEGURIDAD

Toronto se encuentra entre las ciudades más seguras del mundo. Sin embargo, los visitantes siempre deberían tener cautela en lugares desconocidos.

Seguridad personal

- Siempre que sea posible, viaja en grupo y ponte de acuerdo con los demás para que dentro del grupo cada uno se asegure de que el otro no corra peligro.
- Camina con confianza y mira qué o quién está a tu alrededor en todo momento.
- Camina por áreas bien iluminadas, preferentemente del mismo lado de la calle donde están las luces.
- Después de que oscureció, evita los atajos por estacionamientos vacíos, callejones, parques o patios de escuelas.
- Si sospechas que alguien te está siguiendo, ve al área pública más cercana y llama a la policía marcando el 911.
- En bares o discotecas, *nunca* descuides tu bebida ni aceptes pastillas de nadie.

Seguridad de tus objetos personales

- Personaliza tu mochila de la JMJ y otros bolsos con algo que puedas reconocer fácilmente. Esto puede ser la bandera de tu país, insignias coleccionables o algún material de color distintivo.
- Pon la identificación del equipaje tanto dentro como fuera de tu mochila y de otros bolsos. Sólo pon tu nombre y país de origen en la identificación. No incluyas información personal. Utiliza candados para asegurar los bolsos con cierre.
- Pon etiquetas con tu nombre a la ropa.
- Lleva siempre contigo las medicinas que te han sido recetadas.
- No lleves contigo grandes cantidades de dinero. Utiliza

cheques de viajero o tarjetas de crédito, siempre que sea posible. Es más seguro llevar una riñonera (canguro) que un monedero o billetera.

- Nunca dejes tus objetos personales solos, especialmente en el aeropuerto, en estaciones de autobuses o de trenes.
- Siempre que sea posible, deja tus documentos de viaje y objetos de valor en un lugar seguro donde estás alojado. No los lleves a los eventos.
- Fotocopia todos los documentos de viaje importantes como pasaporte y pasajes de avión. Anota los números de serie de tus cheques de viajero y equipos electrónicos, y los números de cuenta de tus tarjetas de crédito. De inmediato, avisa la pérdida o robo de documentos de viaje o personales a un policía o a un voluntario que te puede guiar hacia el oficial de policía más cercano.

Seguridad contra incendios

Para reducir el riesgo de incendio:

- Se prohíben las llamas abiertas, incluso encender velas, en todas las áreas de tu hospedaje.
- Mantén las velas encendidas lejos de materiales inflamables y nunca descuides una vela.
- Si observas algo que pueda provocar un incendio, llama al (416) 338-9050.

Si descubres fuego:

- Sal del lugar inmediatamente y ayuda a salir a toda persona que esté en peligro.
- Activa la alarma de incendio y avisa al personal.
- Sigue las instrucciones de la lista a continuación.

Si oyes una alarma de incendio en un edificio:

- Obedece las instrucciones del personal del edificio.
- Sal del edificio de inmediato.

- Cierra todas las puertas que cruces al salir.
- Utiliza las escaleras para salir del edificio. No uses los ascensores.
- Dirígete al área externa de encuentro designada. No vuelvas a ingresar al edificio.

PÉRDIDA O ROBO DE PASAPORTE O VISA

Debes denunciar a la estación de policía más cercana la pérdida o robo de pasaportes. También deberías contactar al consulado o embajada de tu país para denunciar la pérdida y obtener un reemplazo. La lista de Embajadas y Consulados que se encuentra al final de este libro contiene la información que necesitas para ponerte en contacto con los funcionarios de tu país.

OBJETOS PERDIDOS

El Toronto Police Service (Servicio de Policía de Toronto) operará oficinas de Objetos Perdidos en el Exhibition Place y en el Parque Downsview. En estos lugares, puedes denunciar una pérdida o llevar un objeto que encontraste.

BOLSO DEL PEREGRINO

Dentro de tu mochila, encontrarás:
- Un mapa de Toronto
- Un prendedor de la JMJ
- Una pañoleta de la JMJ
- Velas
- Un portavelas
- Una cruz
- Un rosario
- Un prendedor de Canadá
- Una bandera de Canadá

– Etiquetas para identificación del equipaje
– Postales

Nota: Cuando recibas tu mochila, también te darán el Libro de Liturgia, el Manual del Peregrino y tu Pase.

TU PASE

- Tu Pase te permite participar en todos los eventos de la JMJ. También te permite utilizar el sistema de transporte público de Toronto sin costo alguno durante la JMJ.
- Por favor, completa el Pase con los datos importantes que se solicitan. Encontrarás los teléfonos de emergencia y de información de la JMJ en el Pase.
- Por favor, haz que la JMJ sea un éxito llevando el Pase contigo en un lugar visible en todo momento.
- El borde de color de tu Pase es del mismo color de tu sección asignada en el Parque Downsview.
- Si pierdes tu Pase, dirígete a la Cabina de Información de la JMJ o al centro de inscripción para que te ayuden.

COMPORTAMIENTO APROPIADO

Mientras estás en Toronto, tu comportamiento afecta a todos los jóvenes católicos. Si muestras un comportamiento ofensivo que perturba el desarrollo de las actividades oficiales, serás expulsado.

HOSPEDAJE

En cada lugar de hospedaje de la JMJ, habrá equipos capacitados para ayudarte. Estos voluntarios son tus anfitriones. Sigue todas las instrucciones de seguridad y comunícales toda inquietud que tengas.

Escuelas y otros hospedajes para grupos

- Siempre tendrás que presentar tu Pase para ingresar a tu sitio de hospedaje.

- Respeta los horarios de llegada y partida que los equipos anfitriones te dan. Los sitios de hospedaje de la JMJ están abiertos para ti de 8 p.m. a 9 a.m. Las instalaciones están cerradas en todo horario fuera del mencionado y no se permitirá el ingreso a nadie. Si te enfermas y no puedes asistir a las actividades del día, te dirigirán a la enfermería de la JMJ más cercana.

- Por favor, utiliza solamente las áreas públicas y mantén los niveles de ruido al mínimo en las áreas donde se duerme. Abstente de comportamiento perturbador y respeta el derecho de tus compañeros peregrinos a la privacidad y a la paz y tranquilidad.

- Está estrictamente prohibido fumar y consumir bebidas alcohólicas en cualquier propiedad de hospedaje de la JMJ. Si violas estas reglas, te expulsarán del lugar de hospedaje inmediatamente, y tendrás que conseguirte otro alojamiento y tendrás que pagarlo.

- Se prohíbe el uso de electrodomésticos y de equipos eléctricos, tales como calentadores de agua o calefactores eléctricos.

- Las instalaciones se cierran a la 1:00 a.m. Por favor, regresa al sitio de tu hospedaje antes de esa hora.

- Todo alimento debe consumirse fuera de la propiedad. No se permiten comidas dentro de la misma.

Casas de familia

- Hospedarse en una casa de familia es un privilegio. Por favor, respeta a los anfitriones que te han acogido en sus hogares.

- Por favor, obedece las reglas de la casa y pedidos del anfitrión con respecto a cuestiones tales como horarios de llegada y de salida.

TRANSPORTE EN TORONTO

Toronto es una ciudad en la cual los visitantes no tienen difi-
cultades para desplazarse y la mayoría de la gente de
Toronto da indicaciones con gusto. Pide ayuda si estás per-
dido o confundido.

Transporte público

- La Toronto Transit Commission (TTC) opera un servicio de
autobuses, tranvías y metro en toda la ciudad. GO Transit
opera un servicio de trenes y autobuses en el Área
Metropolitana de Toronto. También está disponible un servicio de tránsito local en los alrededores del Área
Metropolitana de Toronto.
  - Para información sobre el servicio de TTC, llame al (416)
  393-4636
  - Para información sobre el servicio GO, llame al (416)
  869-3200
- Tu inscripción te da derecho a viajar gratis con el TTC
durante las fechas identificadas en tu inscripción. Para
viajar con el TTC fuera de estas fechas, se aplican las tari-
fas regulares.
- Cuando viajes en metro, autobús o tranvía, por favor
recuerda estos *consejos de seguridad*:
  - En los autobuses, *"Request Stop"* ("Solicitar parada")
  permite a las mujeres que viajan solas entre las 9:00
  p.m. y las 5:00 a.m. pedir al conductor que las deje
  bajar entre paradas.
  - Cuando estés bajando del tranvía, mira hacia la derecha
  antes de poner un pie en la calle. Asegúrate que todo el
  tránsito se haya detenido.
  - En todos las andenes del metro/ Rapid Transit (RT) hay
  "Designated Waiting Areas" (Áreas Designadas de
  Espera). Estas áreas están bien iluminadas y tienen un
  intercomunicador conectado con el personal de la
  estación del TTC.

– En todos los coches del metro/ RT hay *"Passenger Assistance Alarms"* (Alarmas para Asistencia al Pasajero). Presiona esta alarma para avisar de un incendio, acoso, enfermedad, accidentes, actos de vandalismo o cualquier otro incidente que afecte la seguridad del pasajero.

Taxis

• En el centro de Toronto, es fácil parar un taxi en la calle. Si la luz del techo de un taxi está encendida, significa que está disponible. Para llamar un taxi, por favor consulta las Páginas Amarillas de la guía telefónica y ve a la sección *Taxis*.

• Asegúrate de que el taxímetro esté encendido antes de que comience el viaje. Paga la suma indicada en el mismo. Es opcional dar propina.

• Aunque el servicio de taxi está ampliamente disponible en Toronto, puede ser costoso. Un viaje desde el centro a las afueras es caro. Puedes pedirle al recepcionista de la compañía de taxi o al conductor que te dé una tarifa aproximada antes de decidir viajar.

• Todos los conductores de taxi y los taxis de Toronto tienen que tener licencia. La foto del conductor y la información del dueño del taxi debe estar en el taxi en la parte trasera del apoyacabezas. Para quejas e información, comuníquese con el 1-877-868-2947.

Estacionamiento en las calles de Toronto o en propiedad privada

• La policía y las autoridades de estacionamiento controlan *de manera estricta* el estacionamiento en Toronto. Las multas son costosas. Para evitar que una grúa se lleve tu automóvil, obedece todas las señales y no dejes tu auto en ningún lugar a menos que sea un lugar para estacionar.

- Si estacionas en un estacionamiento en el cual no se encuentra ningún empleado, sigue las instrucciones que allí se encuentran, generalmente en un cartel fuera de la cabina o en un letrero grande.
- Para información o quejas sobre estacionamiento, llama al (416) 392-3082.

Conducir en Toronto

- Para información sobre calles, comunícate al (416) 599-9090.
- No hay acceso vehicular al Exhibition Place ni al Parque Downsview durante la JMJ.

SITIOS DE LOS EVENTOS

Ten en cuenta que las radio de emisión y recepción y las radios tipo *walkie-talkie* están prohibidas en todos los sitios y serán deshabilitadas apenas sean detectadas. Por favor, utiliza teléfonos celulares si necesitas comunicarte.

Exhibition Place

El Exhibition Place, ubicado cerca del centro de Toronto justo al norte del Lago Ontario, está abierto de 9:00 a.m. a 10 p.m. del lunes 22 de julio al jueves 25 de julio, y desde las 9:00 a.m. a las 6:00 p.m. el viernes 26 de julio.

El Exhibition Place es el lugar donde se llevan a cabo las catequesis desde el miércoles 24 de julio al viernes 26 de julio. Durante las tardes, en un área cercana, el Parque Duc in Altum, se celebra el Sacramento de la Reconciliación. Durante las tardes y noches, el Exhibition Place también es sede del Festival Juvenil.

Todos los participantes concurren al Exhibition Place para la **Ceremonia de Bienvenida Papal** el jueves 25 de julio a las 5:00 p.m.

Ten en cuenta que los siguientes objetos y actividades están prohibidos en el Exhibition Place:

- propano
- asadores
- acampar
- patines
- bicicletas
- monopatines
- patinetas
- botellas de vidrio
- bebidas alcohólicas
- fuegos artificiales

Todas las cosas que poseas pueden ser inspeccionadas.

University Avenue

La University Avenue es una de las calles principales de Toronto. La ceremonia del **Vía Crucis** comenzará en la Plaza Nathan Phillips, delante de la Alcaldía de Toronto el viernes 26 de julio a las 7:30 p.m. Continuará hacia el norte de la University Avenue, pasará por la Legislatura de la Provincia de Ontario y la Universidad de Toronto, y terminará en el Royal Ontario Museum cerca de la intersección de Bloor Street West y Avenue Road.

Parque Downsview

Los peregrinos irán al Parque Downsview en el noroeste de Toronto, ubicado a 15 km del Exhibition Place, el sábado 27 de julio. Por favor, ten en cuenta que *no* se te permitirá el ingreso al Parque Downsview antes de las 8 a.m. del sábado 27 de julio. Se te asignará una de cuatro rutas para caminar, cada una de alrededor de 8 km.

Participarás en una **Vigilia con el Papa**, que incluirá oraciones, canciones, lecturas de la Sagrada Escritura, testimonios y un mensaje del Papa, y comenzará a las 7:30 p.m. del 27 de julio. Después de la Vigilia, el Papa se irá del Parque para pasar la noche y tú dormirás en el Parque Downsview al aire libre.

El domingo 28 de julio, el Papa celebrará Misa a las 9:30 a.m. para concluir la JMJ. La Misa está abierta a todo el público. Por favor, quédate en el lugar al menos una hora después de que haya terminado la **Misa Papal**, para que el público tenga la oportunidad de salir primero. La JMJ, asimismo, te pide que recojas la basura y la deposites en los cestos apropiados para la misma o en las bolsas que te darán. *Debes* haberte ido del Parque Downsview para las 9:00 p.m. del 28 de julio.

Ten en cuenta que todos los objetos y actividades prohibidas en el Exhibition Place también lo están en el Parque Downsview, con la excepción de acampar durante la noche del sábado 27 de julio.

COMIDAS

Plan de comidas completo

El plan de comidas completo incluye 11 comidas. Comienza con la cena del martes 23 de julio y termina con el almuerzo del domingo 28 de julio.

Plan de comidas para el fin de semana

El plan de comidas para el fin de semana incluye tres comidas: la cena del sábado 27 de julio y el desayuno y almuerzo del domingo 28 de julio.

Menús

Los menús reflejan una amplia gama de cocinas de diversas culturas. De las 11 comidas del programa de comidas completo, ocho incluyen un plato caliente. Te entregarán comidas frías en caja para que puedas asistir a los eventos en la ciudad sin tener que regresar a tu puesto de comida.

El menú se basa en la *Canada's Food Guide to Healthy Eating* (Guía Alimentaria de Canadá para una Alimentación Sana) y cumple los requisitos nutricionales que ahí se delinean.

En cada comida está disponible una opción de menú vegetariano.

Horarios y sitios de comidas

Tanto en el Exhibition Place como en el Parque Downsview hay pabellones de comida. La ubicación de tu puesto de comida se basa en el lugar que te han asignado para tu catequesis.

Martes 23 de julio

- La **cena** se sirve después de la Misa de Apertura y Bienvenida, aproximadamente a las 6:30 p.m., y continúa hasta las 10:00 p.m.

Miércoles 24 de julio

- El **almuerzo** comienza después de las catequesis, aproximadamente a las 12:30 p.m., y continúa hasta las 2:30 p.m.
- La **cena** comienza a las 5:30 p.m. y continúa hasta las 8:00 p.m.

Jueves 25 de julio

- El **almuerzo** comienza después de la catequesis, aproximadamente a las 12:30 p.m., y continúa hasta las 2:30 p.m.
- La **cena** se servirá en el Exhibition Place después de la Ceremonia de Bienvenida Papal desde las 6:30 p.m. hasta las 10 p.m.

Viernes 26 de julio

- El **almuerzo** comienza después de la catequesis, aproximadamente a las 12:30 p.m., y continúa hasta las 2:30 p.m.
- Una **cena** fría **en caja** está disponible en tu puesto de comida asignado para que lo recojas durante la hora de almuerzo para que todos puedan participar del Vía Crucis.

Sábado 27 de julio

- Desde las 8:30 a.m. hasta las 4:00 p.m., se distribuye a

los peregrinos el **almuerzo en cajas** a lo largo de la ruta que se les ha asignado para la peregrinación.

Servicio de comidas en el Parque Downsview

El plan de comidas en el Parque Downsview, incluso el Plan de Comidas para el fin de semana, cubre las tres comidas siguientes:

Sábado 27 de julio

- La **cena** comienza a las 4:00 p.m. y continúa hasta las 7:00 p.m.

Domingo 28 de julio

- El **desayuno** comienza a las 5:00 a.m. y continúa hasta las 8:00 a.m.
- El **almuerzo** comienza después de la Misa Papal, alrededor de las 12:30 p.m., y continúa hasta las 3:00 p.m.

Entrega de comidas

Tu paquete de inscripción incluye unos boletos de colores para las comidas; los colores te ayudan a identificar los lugares para obtener tus comidas. Símbolos reconocidos internacionalmente, junto al texto en inglés, francés, español e italiano, indican los sitios donde se sirve la comida.

La comida se servirá en grupos de seis. Sólo una persona del grupo recogerá toda la comida para las seis personas.

Necesidades alimentarias especiales

Vegetarianas: En cada comida en todos los pabellones, se ofrece una opción vegetariana.

Alergias: Todos los menús están preparados usando al mínimo los alérgenos alimenticios más comunes, aunque pueden estar presentes cantidades mínimas de los mismos. Por los problemas de alergias, todo alimento que contenga frutas secas está claramente identificado en las etiquetas de los envases.

Una lista completa de los ingredientes se encuentra disponible en cada pabellón de comidas. Las personas que tengan alergias a alimentos deberían hablar con los encargados de los pabellones.

Otros servicios de comida

Tanto en el Exhibition Place y en el Parque Downsview, las concesiones ofrecen una variedad de alimentos de muchas culturas. Trae algo de dinero contigo si te gustaría probar algunos de los alimentos y bebidas deliciosos que están disponibles.

Agua

Con cada comida, recibes una botella de agua de 500 ml. Puedes rellenar tu botella de agua sin costo alguno en las estaciones de relleno en el Exhibition Place, a lo largo de las rutas de Peregrinación y en el Parqué Downsview. Deberías tomar agua durante todo el día, y aprovechar toda oportunidad para rellenar tu botella de agua. Puedes comprar agua y otras bebidas frías en el Exhibition Place y en el Parque Downsview, y en toda la ciudad.

CRONOGRAMA DE EVENTOS

El programa te da la oportunidad de vivir la Iglesia por medio de encuentros con el Papa, con los pastores de la Iglesia y otros peregrinos.

Los encuentros principales con todos los participantes son los siguientes:

- **Misa de Apertura y Bienvenida** el martes 23 de julio a las 5:00 p.m. en el Exhibition Place
- **Ceremonia de Bienvenida Papal** el jueves 25 de julio a las 5:00 p.m. en el Exhibition Place
- **Vía Crucis** el viernes 26 de julio a las 7:30 p.m. por la University Avenue

- **Vigilia con el Papa** el sábado 27 de julio a las 7:30 p.m. en el Parque Downsview
- **Misa Papal** el domingo 28 de julio a las 9:30 a.m. en el Parque Downsview

---

Lunes 22 de julio

Llegada a Toronto

Llegas al Área Metropolitana de Toronto, te ubicas en tu lugar de hospedaje y conoces a los jóvenes quienes, junto con las iglesias locales y toda la comunidad, serán tus anfitriones.

Martes 23 de julio

Misa de Apertura y Bienvenida
Tarde/Noche

- Su Eminencia Aloysius Cardenal Ambrozic, Arzobispo de Toronto, celebra la Eucaristía en el Exhibition Place a las 5:00 p.m.
- Concierto de Apertura en el que actuarán talentos canadienses en el Exhibition Place.
- Sacramento de la Reconciliación

Miércoles 24 de julio

Mañana

- Catequesis (momentos de oración, debates y reflexión basados en las enseñanzas de los obispos de todo el mundo)
- Una Misa concluye las catequesis.

Tarde y noche

- Servicio Social
- Festival Juvenil que consiste en actividades espirituales, culturales y de entretenimiento
- Sacramento de la Reconciliación

Jueves 25 de julio

Ceremonia de Bienvenida Papal

Mañana

- Catequesis (ver miércoles)

Tarde

- Ceremonia de Bienvenida Papal en el Exhibition Place a las 5:00 p.m.
- Sacramento de la Reconciliación

Noche

- Festival Juvenil
- Sacramento de la Reconciliación

Viernes 26 de julio

Vía Crucis

Mañana

- Catequesis (igual que en los días anteriores)

Tarde

- Servicio Social
- Festival Juvenil
- STREETFEST!
- Sacramento de la Reconciliación

Noche

- Vía Crucis por la University Avenue a las 7:30 p.m.

Sábado 27 de julio

Mañana y tarde

- Misa matutina a las 8:00 a.m. en las parroquias en todo Toronto
- Peregrinación a pie hacia el Parque Downsview

– Concierto de bienvenida en el Parque Downsview
– Sacramento de la Reconciliación

Vigilia con el Papa
Noche

– La Vigilia comienza a las 7:30 p.m. con oración, música, testimonios y un mensaje del Papa.
– El Papa se va después de la Vigilia y tú duermes al aire libre en el Parque Downsview.

Domingo 28 de julio

Misa Papal

– Desde las 9:30 a.m. hasta el mediodía, el Papa celebra Misa en el Parque Downsview. Este evento está abierto a todo el público.

IDIOMAS PARA INTERPRETACIÓN SIMULTÁNEA

La interpretación simultánea por radio está disponible en la:

- Misa de Apertura y Bienvenida el 23 de julio
- Ceremonia de Bienvenida Papal el 25 de julio
- Vía Crucis el 26 de julio
- Vigilia con el Papa el 27 de julio
- Misa Papal el 28 de julio

La información contenida en la siguiente tabla está sujeta a cambios.

Idioma	Frecuencia – banda FM	Idioma	Frecuencia – banda FM
Inglés	104.9	Francés	103.9
Español	101.7	Italiano	102.7
Portugués	99.5	Polaco	91.9
Alemán	90.7	Árabe	98.7

FESTIVAL JUVENIL

El Festival Juvenil congrega a jóvenes para que muestren sus tradiciones, culturas, idiomas y vivencias. Tiene lugar en las noches del 23 de julio al 25 de julio, y en las tardes del 24 y 25 de julio. Los eventos incluyen lo siguiente:

Presentaciones

Quinientas presentaciones de música, danzas, teatro y películas tendrán lugar en 25 escenarios.

STREETFEST!

Durante la tarde del viernes 26 de julio, artistas callejeros se presentan a lo largo de la University Avenue.

Oración

La amplia variedad de momentos de oración y de alabanza estará representada en las iglesias de Toronto y en otros lugares.

Exposiciones

En el Exhibition Place, habrá exposiciones sobre temas de arte, cultura, vocaciones, servicio social y justicia social.

Seminarios

En muchos lugares, habrá foros de discusión sobre una amplia gama de temas.

Encuentros

En iglesias y parques, habrá oportunidades de reunirse y celebrar basándose en una espiritualidad, idioma o etnia común.

Cafés

Habrá debates informales en cafés, algunos de los cuales tendrán acceso a Internet.

Actividades vocacionales

El Pabellón de Vocación y Servicio en el Exhibition Place

ofrece un lugar en el cual puedes reflexionar sobre un posible llamado de Dios. También te ofrecerá la oportunidad de conocer a otras personas, de hablar y celebrar con ellos.

Festival de Cine

Se pasará una selección de películas de temas religiosos, incluso el estreno mundial del documental sobre la Madre Teresa.

Imágenes de Salvación

El Royal Ontario Museum (ROM) está presentando *Imágenes de Salvación*, que contiene más de 100 piezas de los Museos Vaticanos y otras colecciones italianas. El ROM se encuentra en Queen's Park 100, en la intersección de Bloor Street West y Avenue Road, junto a la estación de metro Museum. El horario extendido del ROM desde el 21 al 27 de julio es de 10:00 a.m. a 9:30 p.m. Presentando tu pase de la JMJ, recibirás un descuento y la entrada te costará $5.

Actividades recreativas

Algunos parques de Toronto ofrecerán actividades para quienes deseen participar en juegos o deportes.

Servicio Social

Tienes la posibilidad de participar en actividades de servicio social para dejar un legado de cuidado a los demás y para demostrar nuestra fe con nuestros hermanos y hermanas de todos los credos. Los grupos que se han inscrito para el Servicio Social asistirán a una sesión de tres horas de 2:30 a 5:30 p.m. el miércoles 24 de julio y el viernes 26 de julio.

Existen tres tipos de actividades de servicio social:

- Proyectos de servicio que ayudan de manera directa a las personas
- Debates sobre temas de servicio específicos
- Visitas a organizaciones de servicio locales

Catequesis

Las catequesis tienen lugar el miércoles 24 de julio, jueves 25 de julio y viernes 26 de julio y están organizadas por grupos de idioma en muchos sitios. Los obispos de todo el mundo conducen estas sesiones, que se llevarán a cabo a la mañana, sobre las enseñanzas de la fe católica, que incluyen la participación en los sacramentos de la Sagrada Eucaristía y de la Reconciliación.

Los temas son los siguientes:

Miércoles: *Vosotros Sois la Sal de la Tierra*

Jueves: *Vosotros Sois la Luz del Mundo*

Viernes: *Reconciliaos con Dios*

Sacramento de la Reconciliación

Tendrás tres ocasiones para participar del Sacramento de la Reconciliación:

- Los sacerdotes están disponibles durante las mañanas del miércoles 24 de julio al viernes 26 de julio en los sitios de las catequesis.
- En el Parque Duc in Altum, justo al este de las puertas principales del Exhibition Place, cientos de sacerdotes están disponibles:
  - Martes 23 de julio de las 2:00 p.m. a las 4:00 p.m. y de las 6:00 p.m. a las 8:00 p.m.
  - Miércoles 24 de julio de las 2:00 p.m. a las 8:00 p.m.
  - Jueves 25 de julio de las 2:00 p.m. a las 4:00 p.m. y de las 6:00 p.m. a las 8:00 p.m.
  - Viernes 26 de julio de las 2:00 p.m. a las 6:00 p.m.
- El sábado 27 de julio en el Parque Downsview, los sacerdotes están disponibles desde las 2:00 p.m. hasta el comienzo de la Vigilia con el Papa.

Yes! I want to remember WYD 2002

ORDER FORM

Title	Qty	Price $
World Youth Day 2002 *Official Souvenir Album*		**$21.95** (reg. $29.95)
Pope John Paul II speaks to a new generation, 1985 – 2002 *Be Not Afraid!*		**$12.95**
	Subtotal	
	Shipping	
	GST (7%)	
	TOTAL (AJM)	

Mode of Payment:
☐ Cheque or money order
OR charge my:
☐ VISA ☐ MASTERCARD

Shipping & Handling
(higher outside Canada)
Up to $50: $3.95
$50 - $99: $6.95/ $100+ 7% of Total

Card No.: _____
Expiry Date: _____
Signature _____
(required)

Ship to Name: _____
Address: _____
City: _____
Prov./State. _____ *Postal code:* _____
Country _____
Tel. no.: ( ) _____

Other ways to order— e: youth@novalis.ca
t: 1-800-387-7164 • fax: 1-800-204-4140
NOVALIS, 49 Front St. East, Toronto, ON Canada M5E 1B3

WORLD YOUTH DAY 2002
THE OFFICIAL SOUVENIR ALBUM

TORONTO, CANADA
July 18-28, 2002

Be not afraid!

World Youth Day 1985-200

Offre spéciale aux participants

JOURNÉE MONDIALE DE LA JEUNESSE 2002
L'ALBUM SOUVENIR OFFICIEL

TORONTO, CANADA
18-28 juillet 2002

BON DE COMMANDE

Titre	Qté	Prix
Jean-Paul II parle aux jeunes *N'ayez pas peur ! 4056807*		15,95 $*
Journée mondiale de la jeunesse 2002 *L'album souvenir officiel 4078006*		25,50 $*
	TOTAL	

JMA

Mode de paiement
* TPS et frais de transport inclus
☐ Chèque
☐ Mandat poste
Cartes de crédit
☐ VISA ☐ MASTERCARD

N° carte _____

Date d'expiration _____

Signature _____

EXPÉDIER À :

Nom _____

Adresse _____

Ville _____

Province _____ Pays _____

Téléphone (___) _____

Commande téléphonique: **1-800-668-2547**   Courrier électronique: **sac@novalis-inc.com**

1000056512-H2H2T1-BR01

NOVALIS
CP 990 SUCC DELORIMIER
MONTRÉAL QC H2H 9Z9

TIENDA DE LA JMJ

Puedes comprar artículos oficiales en tres sitios. La tienda de la JMJ está ubicada en Yonge Street N° 433, cerca de la estación de metro College. En Exhibition Place y en el Parque Downsview, hay pabellones de venta donde puedes comprar recuerdos, libros, música y ropa.

VOLUNTARIOS

- Los voluntarios están en todos los eventos para ayudarte a ti y a los organizadores de los eventos. También se encuentran en las Cabinas de Información de la JMJ ubicadas en toda la ciudad.

- Los voluntarios pueden comunicarse en los cuatro idiomas oficiales de la JMJ: inglés, francés, español e italiano. No dudes en pedir ayuda a los voluntarios.

- Los voluntarios están vestidos con camisas azules con el logo que se muestra a continuación.

RESPETO AL MEDIOAMBIENTE

- Cajas de cartón especialmente señaladas están disponibles para botellas, latas y para los desechos de papel tales como diarios, revistas, envoltorios de alimento limpios. Bolsas de papel grandes están disponibles para los restos de comida. Por favor, sigue las instrucciones de las cajas y bolsas, y recicla siempre que sea posible.

- En el Parque Downsview, se necesita tu ayuda para mover los contenedores de reciclaje llenos a la calle para su recolección y luego para que regreses contenedores vacíos a tu área para que sean llenados.

- Siempre que sea posible, por favor levanta la basura y ponla en el contenedor apropiado.

- En la mayoría de las calles principales, hay contenedores disponibles para desechos y para reciclaje.

TELÉFONOS

- Una llamada local desde un teléfono público cuesta 25 centavos ($0,25). Los números de teléfono canadienses tienen un mínimo de siete dígitos, pero algunas ciudades más grandes, incluso Toronto y los alrededores, requieren un código de área de tres dígitos adicional para llamadas locales. Los códigos de área para Toronto son 416 y 647. Para el Área Metropolitana de Toronto, los códigos de área son 905 y 289.

- Para las llamadas de larga distancia dentro de Canadá y desde Canadá a los Estados Unidos tienes que marcar 1 + código de área + número local. Para llamar a otros países, tienes que marcar 011 + código de país + código de ciudad + número local. Para una llamada directa (de persona a persona), con tarjeta telefónica (Calling Card), a pagar por un tercero y por cobrar, a través de la operadora, marca 01 + código de país + código de ciudad + número local. En la primera sección de las páginas blancas de la guía telefónica, se encuentra un listado de los códigos de los países.

- Puedes comprar tarjetas telefónicas oficiales de la JMJ de $10 y $20 en los sitios de inscripción de la JMJ, en el Parque Downsview y en el Exhibition Place. Hay 12 tarjetas de la serie para coleccionar. Puedes utilizarlas para realizar llamadas a todo el mundo desde Canadá y Estados Unidos.

- Puedes también alquilar teléfonos celulares en muchos lugares.

ACCESO A INTERNET

- Las 98 sucursales de las Bibliotecas Públicas de Toronto [*Toronto Public Libraries*, TPL] ofrecen acceso a Internet de alta velocidad gratis.

- La principal sucursal de la TPL, la *Toronto Reference Library* (ubicada en Yonge Street N° 789, una cuadra al norte de Bloor Street), tiene más de 100 computadoras y más de 100 diarios de todo el mundo.

- Para mayor información, llama a la Línea de Información de la TPL al (416) 393-7131.

- El acceso a Internet está disponible en algunos cafés del Festival Juvenil.

ELECTRICIDAD

Canadá tiene la norma eléctrica de 110 volts, a diferencia de Europa y muchos países de todo el mundo, que utilizan la norma de 220-240 volts.

DINERO E IMPUESTOS

- La moneda canadiense utiliza dólares y centavos. El dólar estadounidense ofrece una tasa de cambio favorable.

- Para conseguir la mejor tasa de cambio, cambia tu dinero en una institución financiera reconocida, como un banco, una institución fiduciaria o una casa de cambio.

- A las monedas de Canadá de un dólar y de dos por lo general se las llama *loonie* y *toonie*, respectivamente. Cada valor de papel moneda tiene su propio color y diseño. Muchos negocios no aceptan billetes de $50 o más.

Impuestos canadienses a las ventas

El Impuesto sobre Productos y Servicios (GST, siglas en inglés) es un impuesto federal de un 7 por ciento que se aplica a la mayoría de los bienes y servicios. Toronto, como parte de la provincia de Ontario, también tiene un impuesto provincial sobre las ventas (PST, siglas en inglés) de 8 por ciento que se aplicará a la mayoría de los bienes que adquieras.

Reembolso de Impuesto a los Visitantes

- Los visitantes no residentes en Canadá tienen derecho a un reembolso del Impuesto sobre Productos y Servicios aplicado a ciertos bienes adquiridos en Canadá que se lleven del país, como así también aplicado a hospedaje por períodos breves.

- Guarda los recibos de tus compras y de tu hospedaje, si deseas solicitar un reembolso del Impuesto sobre Productos y Servicios. Puedes conseguir una copia de la Solicitud de Reembolso de Impuestos a Visitantes (*Tax Refund Application for Visitors*) en cualquier oficina de Aduanas de Canadá o en la mayoría de los centros de información turística, tiendas *duty-free*, tiendas departamentales y algunos hoteles.

- Los Reembolsos de Impuestos a Visitantes también pueden obtenerse en muchas cabinas del Parque Downsview y del Exhibition Place. Trae tus recibos de compra e identificación que demuestre que no vives en Canadá para un procesamiento rápido del reembolso.

Tarjetas de crédito / Cajeros Automático

- Se aceptan con facilidad las principales tarjetas de crédito tales como Visa, MasterCard, American Express y Diners Club. Tu institución financiera automáticamente convertirá los dólares canadienses en la divisa de tu país en tu resumen mensual.

- La mayoría de los cajeros automáticos canadienses (ABMs, siglas en inglés) aceptan la tarjeta de débito de los sistemas Interac, Cirrus y Plus. Además de en los bancos, encontrarás cajeros automáticos en aeropuertos, algunos edificios gubernamentales y en muchas tiendas.

- Si pierdes tu tarjeta de crédito o de débito, inmediatamente contacta a tu institución financiera y denuncia la pérdida a la policía.

SERVICIOS POSTALES

- Si quieres comprar estampillas, se venden en muchas farmacias, almacenes, además de en los puntos oficiales de venta del Correo (Canada Post).

- Puedes enviar cartas o postales depositándolas en los buzones de Canada Post, que se encuentran en la mayoría de las intersecciones principales o cerca de ellas.

- Si necesitas otro tipo de servicio postal, tal como enviar un paquete o una carta certificada, tendrás que dirigirte a un punto de venta de Canada Post. Éstos se encuentran en ciertas tiendas, tales como farmacias, tiendas de productos de oficina, entre otras. Los negocios que cuentan con un punto de venta de Canada Post tienen el logo de Canada Post (que se muestra a continuación) en sus carteles o en sus vidrieras.

- Las cartas simples, incluso las postales, cuestan: $0,48 dentro de Canadá, $0,65 a los Estados Unidos y $1,25 a todos los demás países.

From anywhere...   De partout...
to anyone   jusqu'à vous

ITALIANO

INDICE

SIMBOLI

Raccolta Differenziata

Pronto Soccorso Pellegrini

Ospedale Regionale/Comunale

Sicurezza

Iscrizioni

Acqua Potabile

Acqua Non Potabile

Servizio di Ristorazione

WC

Informazioni

Punto di Ristoro

WC Uomini

Fermata Autobus

TAXI

Punto di Ritrovo Disabili

WC Donne

Palco

Accesso Senza Assistenza

Negozi

Pericolo alta Tensione

Danger

Accesso Con Assistenza

Oggetti smarriti

Attenzione

Area Riservata ai Disabili

Telefono

BÉNÉVOLE WYD2002JMJ VOLUNTEER Volontari

WC Disabili

Punto di Ritrovo Pellegrini

Toronto Transit Commission

Area di Riposo Disabili

Internet

GO Transit

SERVIZIO SANITARIO

Assistenza Medica

*In caso di emergenza medica, chiamate il **911** in qualsiasi momento ovunque vi troviate.*

Questo numero può essere composto gratuitamente da qualsiasi telefono. Informate il Servizio di Emergenza che siete partecipanti della GMG e dite dove siete. L'operatore vi darà opportune istruzioni.

Luoghi della GMG

- Avvertite un qualsiasi volontario o paramedico della GMG. I volontari che portano una maglietta rossa con una croce bianca sono assistenti sanitari qualificati.
- Andate al più vicino punto di assistenza medica della GMG segnato con una croce bianca dentro un cerchio rosso.

In Tutta Toronto

- Avvertite il vostro capo gruppo o chi vi ospita, i quali vi indicheranno il centro medico più vicino.
- Quando cercate assistenza medica, andate sempre in compagnia di qualcuno.
- Quando andate in una clinica o in un ospedale, dite sempre al personale medico che siete partecipanti della GMG.
- Portate sempre con voi il numero di assicurazione. Conservate le ricevute mediche.

Precauzioni al sole

L'estate a Toronto può essere estremamente calda e umida. Per proteggervi dal sole e dal calore:

- Usate il cappello e cercate zone in ombra o fatevi ombra con un ombrello.
- Usate vestiti il più coprenti possibile.
- Usate occhiali da sole con protezione UVA e UVB.

- Usate una lozione solare con fattore di protezione (SPF) 15 o anche più alto. Applicatelo ogni due o tre ore.
- Vestitevi a strati per adattarvi agli sbalzi di temperatura che possono verificarsi nel corso della giornata.
- Bevete molta acqua e portate sempre con voi una bottiglia d'acqua.
- L'acqua del rubinetto a Toronto è potabile. Anche l'acqua in bottiglia è disponibile ovunque.

Leggi sul Fumo e sul Consumo di Alcolici a Toronto

- A Toronto, come in tutta la regione dell'Ontario, è permesso bere alcolici a partire dai 19 anni di età. Il consumo di alcolici è vietato al di fuori di bar e ristoranti, salvo nelle aree esterne appartenenti ai locali, appositamente designate a tale scopo.
- 19 anni è l'età minima per comprare sigarette o altri prodotti da tabacco.
- E' vietato fumare all'interno delle scuole o nei cortili delle scuole, o all'interno della maggior parte degli edifici pubblici. Prima di accendere una sigaretta in pubblico, accertatevi che sia permesso fumare.
- In molti ristoranti a Toronto è vietato fumare; è permesso fumare solo in quei ristoranti muniti di un'apposita sala interna per fumatori. E' permesso fumare nei bar, salvo diverse disposizioni. Nei ristoranti in cui è permesso fumare senza restrizioni di spazio, è vietato l'accesso ai minori di 19 anni.

Ulteriori Suggerimenti Sanitari

- Occasionalmente, è possibile che il dipartimento di sanità pubblica della Città di Toronto lanci un *allarme inquinamento atmosferico*, per indicare la scarsa qualità dell'aria. Se soffrite di asma, allergie, malattie cardiache o polmonari, fate particolare attenzione a non fare sforzi eccessivi. Rallentate l'attività fisica, rinfrescatevi e bevete molta acqua. Se non vi sentite bene, contattate un medico.

- Tutte le spiagge di Toronto sono provviste di segnali indicanti la balneabilità. Alcune zone balneabili non sono controllate da guardaspiaggia. Nuotate sempre in compagnia e attenetevi alle istruzioni segnalate.

- Se venite morsi o graffiati da un animale, avvertite il vostro capo gruppo, chi vi ospita o un membro dello staff o volontario della GMG. Lavate la ferita con acqua calda e sapone e pulitela accuratamente. Rivolgetevi ad un medico.

PELLEGRINI CON BISOGNI PARTICOLARI

Gli eventi, le cerimonie e le celebrazioni della GMG sono state pianificate e organizzate per permettere la partecipazione, nel limite del possibile, di pellegrini con bisogni particolari. Nei luoghi degli eventi verranno esposti i simboli riconosciuti a livello internazionale per assistere e indirizzare le persone con bisogni particolari.

Necessità di Trasporto Particolari

La GMG ha fatto il possibile per garantire il trasporto agli eventi ai pellegrini con disabilità motorie. I pellegrini con disabilità motorie avranno però bisogno di provvedere autonomamente al trasporto per le escursioni che esulano il programma della GMG. Alcune ditte che forniscono mezzi di trasporto accessibili ai disabili sono: Wheel-Trans (416) 393-4222; Royal Taxi Services (416) 955-0564; Beck Taxi (416) 751-5555; TPT (416) 209-0950 e Able Atlantic Taxi (416) 291-4363.

SICUREZZA

Toronto è una delle città più sicure al mondo, ma i turisti dovrebbero sempre fare attenzione in luoghi non familiari.

Sicurezza Personale

- Quando è possibile, viaggiate in gruppo e usate il "buddy system": divisi in coppie, ognuno si assicura che il proprio compagno sia sempre presente.

- Camminate con fare sicuro e siate sempre consapevoli di ciò che vi circonda.
- Camminate in zone ben illuminate, possibilmente nello stesso lato della strada dove sono situati i lampioni.
- Di sera evitate le scorciatoie che attraversano luoghi deserti, vicoli, parchi o cortili di scuole.
- Se sospettate di essere seguiti, raggiungete il posto pubblico più vicino e chiamate la polizia componendo il 911.
- Al bar o in discoteca, non lasciate *mai* le vostre bevande incustodite e non accettate pasticche da nessuno.

Sicurezza degli Effetti Personali

- Personalizzate la vostra Sacca del Pellegrino e le altre borse di vostra proprietà con oggetti facilmente riconoscibili. Utilizzate ad esempio bandierine del vostro paese, distintivi, o altro materiale colorato.
- Mettete etichette di riconoscimento sia dentro che fuori la Sacca del Pellegrino e le altre borse. Nell'etichetta scrivete soltanto il vostro nome ed il paese di provenienza; non aggiungete informazioni personali. Usate lucchetti di sicurezza per chiudere in modo sicuro le borse con cerniera.
- Applicate ai vestiti etichette con il nome.
- Portate sempre con voi i medicinali che vi sono stati prescritti.
- Non portatevi dietro grosse quantità di denaro; non appena possibile, usate traveller's cheques o carte di credito. Il marsupio è spesso più sicuro della borsa o del portafogli.
- Non lasciate mai i vostri effetti personali incustoditi, specialmente in aeroporto, in autobus o nelle stazioni ferroviarie.
- Se possibile, lasciate i documenti di viaggio e gli oggetti di valore al sicuro nel vostro alloggio. Non portateli nei luoghi degli eventi.

- Fotocopiate tutti i documenti di viaggio importanti, come il passaporto ed il biglietto dell'aereo. Annotate i numeri di serie dei vostri traveller's cheques e degli articoli elettronici, ed i numeri di conto delle vostre carte di credito. Denunciate immediatamente la perdita o il furto dei documenti personali o di viaggio alla polizia o ad un volontario che può indirizzarvi all'ufficiale di polizia più vicino.

Sicurezza Antincendi

Precauzioni:

- E' proibito accendere fiamme vive, candele comprese, in tutte le aree dei vostri alloggi.
- Tenete le candele accese lontano da materiali infiammabili e non lasciate mai le candele incustodite.
- Se vi accorgete di un potenziale pericolo di incendio, chiamate il (416) 338-9050.

Se scoprite un incendio:

- Abbandonate l'area immediatamente ed aiutate ad uscire chiunque sia in pericolo.
- Attivate l'allarme anti incendio ed avvertite il personale.
- Attenetevi alle seguenti istruzioni.

Se sentite l'allarme anti incendio in un edificio:

- Seguite le istruzioni del personale dell'edificio.
- Abbandonate immediatamente l'edificio.
- Chiudete tutte le porte dietro di voi.
- Usate le scale per abbandonare l'edificio, non usate gli ascensori.
- Avviatevi alle apposite aree di adunata all'esterno, non rientrate nell'edificio.

PERDITA O FURTO DEL PASSAPORTO O DEL VISTO

E' necessario denunciare la perdita o il furto del passaporto alla più vicina stazione di polizia. Occorre anche contattare il consolato o l'ambasciata del vostro paese per denunciare la perdita del documento ed ottenerne la sostituzione. La lista delle Ambasciate e Consolati in fondo a questa guida riporta tutte le informazioni di cui avete bisogno per contattare i funzionari del vostro paese.

OGGETTI SMARRITI

Il Servizio di Polizia di Toronto metterà in funzione alcuni uffici per gli oggetti smarriti ad Exhibition Place e a Downsview. In questi punti è possibile denunciare uno smarrimento o portare un oggetto trovato.

SACCA DEL PELLEGRINO

All'interno della Sacca del Pellegrino trovate:
– cartina di Toronto
– spilla della GMG
– bandana della GMG
– candele
– bicchiere portacandele
– una croce
– un rosario
– spilla del Canada
– bandiera canadese
– etichette di riconoscimento per il bagaglio
– cartoline

N.B.: Quando riceverete la Sacca del Pellegrino, vi saranno anche consegnati il Libro delle Litrugie, la Guida del Pellegrino ed il Pass.

PASS

- Il Pass vi permette di partecipare a tutti gli eventi della GMG. Vi dà anche la possibilità di usufruire gratuitamente dei trasporti pubblici a Toronto durante la GMG.

- Siete pregati di compilare il Pass con le informazioni importanti richieste. Sul Pass troverete i numeri di emergenza e le Info Line della GMG.

- Vi preghiamo di contribuire alla buona riuscita della GMG indossando sempre il Pass in modo chiaramente visibile.

- Il bordo colorato del vostro Pass indica il colore del settore a Downsview al quale siete stati assegnati.

- Se perdete il Pass, chiedete aiuto ad un Info Point della GMG o al centro iscrizioni.

NORME DI COMPORTAMENTO

Durante la vostra permanenza a Toronto, il vostro comportamento si riperquote su tutti i giovani cattolici. Se mostrerete un comportamento offensivo, che disturba l'andamento di attività ufficiali, sarete allontanati.

ALLOGGI

Presso tutte le strutture di alloggio della GMG sarà disponibile personale addestrato per aiutarvi: i volontari che vi ospiteranno. Seguite tutte le istruzioni di sicurezza e riportate loro qualsiasi perplessità abbiate.

Scuole o Altri Tipi di Alloggio in Gruppo

- Per accedere agli alloggi è sempre necessario indossare il Pass.

- Rispettate gli orari di arrivo e partenza dati dallo staff ospitante. Gli alloggi della GMG sono aperti per voi dalle ore 20:00 alle ore 9:00. Le strutture rimarranno chiuse durante gli altri orari e a nessuno sarà permesso di entrare. Se state male e non potete partecipare alle attività della giornata, verrete condotti alla più vicina infermeria della GMG.

- Siete pregati di utilizzare soltanto le aree pubbliche e di mantenere il massimo silenzio nelle aree di riposo. Astenetevi da comportamenti che potrebbero disturbare e rispettate il diritto alla privacy, pace e tranquillità degli altri pellegrini.

- In tutti gli alloggi della GMG è severamente vietato fumare o consumare bevande alcoliche. Se infrangete queste regole sarete immediatamente allontanati dalla struttura e dovrete trovare una sistemazione alternativa a vostre spese.

- E' proibito l'uso di qualsiasi apparecchiatura elettrica, come ad esempio bollitori o apparecchi per il riscaldamento.

- Le strutture vengono chiuse all'una del mattino. Siete pregati di fare ritorno ai vostri alloggi entro questo orario.

- Il cibo va consumato all'esterno delle strutture. Non è permesso consumare i pasti all'interno.

Alloggi in famiglia

- Essere ospitati in famiglia è un privilegio. Siete pregati di comportarvi in modo rispettoso nei confronti di chi vi ha accolto in casa propria.

- Siete pregati di rispettare le regole di chi vi ospita e di obbedire alle loro richieste riguardo questioni quali gli orari di rientro la sera e di partenza la mattina.

SPOSTARSI A TORONTO

Toronto è una città molto facile da visitare, e la maggior parte dei cittadini è disponibile per dare indicazioni, quindi chiedete aiuto se vi perdete.

Trasporti Pubblici

- La Toronto Transit Commission (TTC) fornisce il servizio di autobus, tram e metropolitana in tutta la città. GO Transit fornisce il servizio treni e autobus nell' Area Metropolitana di Toronto (GTA). Il servizio di trasporto locale è disponibile anche nelle zone che circondano la GTA.

- Per informazioni sul servizio TTC, chiamate il (416) 393-4636
- Per informazioni sul servizio GO, chiamate il (416) 869-3200

• L'iscrizione vi fornisce il trasporto gratuito sui mezzi della TTC per il periodo segnato sul vostro modulo di iscrizione. Per l'uso della TTC al di fuori di tale periodo verranno applicate le normali tariffe.

• Viaggiando in metropolitana, autobus o tram, vi preghiamo di ricordare le seguenti norme di sicurezza:

- In autobus, la dicitura "Request stop" (Fermata a Richiesta) permette alle donne che viaggiano da sole in autobus nella fascia oraria dalle 21:00 e alle 5:00, di chiedere al conducente la possibilità di farle scendere dall'autobus in un punto situato tra le normali fermate della TTC.

- Scendendo dal tram, abbiate l'accortezza di guardare alla vostra destra prima di scendere in strada. Fate attenzione a che il traffico sia completamente fermo.

- Apposite Aree di Attesa si trovano in tutte le piattaforme della metropolitana/Rapid Transit (RT). Tali aree sono ben illuminate e sono fornite di interfono, che permette di comunicare con lo staff della stazione TTC.

- In tutti i treni della metropolitana/RT sono presenti dispositivi di Allarme Assistenza Passeggeri. Suonate l'allarme in caso di incendio, molestie, malore, incidente, atti di vandalismo, o per qualsiasi evento che disturbi i passeggeri.

Taxi

• Nel centro di Toronto è facile trovare un taxi. Se la luce posta sul tetto dell'auto è accesa, significa che il taxi è disponibile. Per chiamare un taxi, consultate le Pagine Gialle sotto la voce "Taxi".

- Assicuratevi che il tassametro sia acceso prima che la corsa inizi. Pagate la somma indicata sul tassametro; la mancia è facoltativa.

- Nonostante il servizio taxi sia largamente disponibile a Toronto, potrebbe risultare caro. Una corsa dal centro città verso la periferia è notevolmente costosa. E' possibile richiedere alla ditta di taxi o all'autista di farvi un preventivo approssimativo della corsa, prima di decidere se usufruire o no del servizio.

- Tutti gli autisti ed i veicoli devono avere regolare licenza per fornire il servizio taxi. La foto dell'autista e le informazioni sul proprietario del taxi devono essere affisse all'interno del veicolo, dietro il poggiatesta. Per lamentele o informazioni, chiamate l'1-877-868-2947.

Parcheggiare sulle strade di Toronto o in Proprietà Private

- Le normative sui parcheggi a Toronto vengono fatte *rigorosamente* rispettare dalla polizia e dalle autorità dei parcheggi e le multe sono molto care. Per evitare che la vostra auto venga rimossa, rispettate i cartelli e non lasciate l'auto parcheggiata in proprietà private, a meno che queste non siano aree apposite per il parcheggio.

- Se lasciate l'auto in un parcheggio non custodito, seguite attentamente le istruzioni affisse.

- Per informazioni o lamentele riguardanti i parcheggi, chiamate il (416) 392-3082.

Guidare a Toronto

- Per informazioni sulle strade, chiamate il (416)-599-9090.

- I veicoli *non* avranno accesso ad Exhibition Place e a Downsview durante la GMG.

UBICAZIONE DEGLI EVENTI

L'uso di apparecchi radio bidirezionali e di walkie-talkie è proibito ovunque durante la GMG, e una volta intercettati, tali apparecchi verranno disabilitati. Per le comunicazioni siete pregati di utilizzare i telefoni cellulari.

Exhibition Place

Exhibition Place, situato vicino al centro di Toronto, a nord del lago Ontario, è aperto dalle ore 9:00 alle ore 22:00 da lunedì 22 luglio a giovedì 25 luglio, e dalle ore 9:00 alle ore 18:00 di venerdì 26 luglio.

Exhibition Place è il luogo delle catechesi da mercoledì 24 luglio a venerdì 26 luglio. Di pomeriggio sarà disponibile, per il Sacramento della Riconciliazione, un'area adiacente ad Exhibition Place, il Parco Duc in Altum. Di pomeriggio e di sera Exhibition Place ospita anche il Festival della Gioventù.

Alle ore 17:00 di giovedì 25 luglio tutti i partecipanti arriveranno ad Exhibition Place per la **Cerimonia d'Accoglienza con il Papa.**

Siete pregati di notare che ad Exhibition Place è vietato portare i seguenti articoli ed esercitare le seguenti attività:

- gas propano
- barbecue
- campeggiare
- roller blades
- biciclette
- monopattino
- skateboard
- bottiglie di vetro
- bevande alcoliche
- fuochi d'artificio

Gli oggetti in vostro possesso potrebbero essere perquisiti.

University Avenue

University Avenue è una delle strade principali di Toronto. La **Via Crucis** partirà alle ore 7:30 di venerdì 26 luglio da Nathan Philips Square, davanti al City Hall (Municipio) di Toronto. Avanzerà verso nord su University Avenue, passerà di fronte alla Sede del Parlamento Provinciale ("Legislature of the Province of Ontario") e davanti all'Università di Toronto, e terminerà davanti al Royal Ontario Museum, vicino all'incrocio tra Bloor Street West e Avenue Road.

Downsview Lands

Sabato 27 luglio i pellegrini convergeranno a Downsview, nella parte nord-est di Toronto, a 15 km da Exhibition Place. *Non* sarà permesso entrare a Downsview prima delle ore 8:00 di sabato 27 luglio. Verrete assegnati ad una delle quattro strade da percorrere a piedi, ognuna lunga circa 8 km.

La sera del 27 luglio, dalle ore 19:30 in poi, parteciperete alla **Veglia con il Papa**, che prevede preghiere, canti, letture delle scritture, testimonianze ed un messaggio da parte del Papa. Dopo la Veglia il Papa lascerà il luogo per la notte, mentre voi pernotterete all'aperto a Downsview.

Domenica 28 luglio il Papa celebrerà la S. Messa alle ore 9:30 del mattino, per la conclusione della GMG. La Messa è aperta al pubblico. Siete pregati di rimanere in loco per almeno un'ora dopo la **Messa Papale**, in modo che i membri del pubblico esterno abbiano l'opportunità di lasciare l'area per primi. La GMG vi prega anche di raccogliere i rifiuti e di depositarli negli appositi cassonetti, o nelle buste che vi verranno date a tale scopo. E' *obbligatorio* che tutti lascino Downsview entro le ore 21:00 di domenica 28 luglio.

N.B.: Gli articoli e le attività proibiti ad Exhibition Place lo sono anche a Downsview, fatta eccezione per la possibilità di campeggiare la notte di sabato 27 luglio.

SERVIZIO DI RISTORAZIONE

Vitto completo

Il vitto completo comprende 11 pasti, a partire dalla cena di martedì 23 luglio e concludendo con il pranzo di domenica 28 luglio.

Vitto del fine settimana

Il vitto del fine settimana copre tre pasti: cena di sabato 27 luglio e colazione e pranzo di domenica 28 luglio.

I menù

I menù riflettono una vasta gamma di cucine di varie culture. Degli 11 pasti del programma "vitto completo", otto sono pasti caldi. Verranno forniti pasti freddi al sacco, in modo che i pellegrini possano partecipare agli eventi per tutta la città senza dover far ritorno ai propri punti di ristorazione.

Il menù si basa sulla Guida del Canada ad una Sana Alimentazione ("Canada's Food Guide to Healthy Eating") ed è conforme alle norme nutrizionali richieste.

Ad ogni pasto è disponibile l'opzione di un menù vegetariano.

Orari e Luoghi della Ristorazione

Ad Exhibition Place e a Downsview sono presenti grandi padiglioni che ospitano il servizio ristorazione. Il vostro punto di Ristorazione si basa sul luogo della catechesi al quale siete stati assegnati.

Martedì 23 luglio

- **La cena** viene servita dopo la Messa di Apertura, alle ore 18:30 circa, e il servizio dura fino alle ore 22:00.

Mercoledì 24 luglio

- **Il pranzo** inizia dopo le catechesi, alle ore 12:30 circa e viene servito fino alle ore 14:30.
- **La cena** inizia alle ore 17:30 e viene servita fino alle ore 20:00.

Giovedì 25 luglio

- **Il pranzo** inizia dopo le catechesi, alle ore 12:30 circa, e viene servito fino alle ore 14:30.
- **La cena** sarà servita ad Exhibition Place dopo la Cerimonia di Accoglienza con il Papa, dalle ore 18:30 alle ore 22:00.

Venerdì 26 luglio

- **Il pranzo** inizia dopo le catechesi, alle ore 12:30 circa, e viene servito fino alle ore 14:30.
- E' disponibile una **cena fredda al sacco** da ritirare al punto di ristorazione a voi assegnato durante le ore del pranzo, per dare la possibilità a tutti di partecipare alla Via Crucis.

Sabato 27 luglio

- **Il pranzo** al sacco è distribuito ai pellegrini lungo la via di pellegrinaggio loro assegnata, dalle ore 8:30 alle ore 16:00.

Servizio di Ristorazione a Downsview

Il servizio di ristorazione a Downsview, comprendente il Vitto del fine settimana, copre i tre pasti seguenti:

Sabato 27 luglio

- **La cena** inizia alle ore 16:00 e viene servita fino alle ore 19:00.

Domenica 28 luglio

- **La colazione** inizia alle ore 5:00 e viene servita fino alle ore 8:00.
- **Il pranzo** inizia dopo la Messa Papale, alle ore 12:30 circa e viene servito fino alle ore 15:00.

Ritiro dei Pasti

Il pacchetto d'iscrizione comprende i buoni pasto, contraddistinti da colori diversi, per aiutarvi ad identificare il luogo dove ritirare i pasti. I luoghi dove viene prestato il Servizio di Ristorazione sono indicati da simboli riconosciuti a livello internazionale, accompagnati dal testo in inglese, francese, spagnolo e italiano.

I pasti saranno consegnati in gruppi di sei, ma ritirati da una sola persona.

Pasti per Diete Particolari

Vegetariani: Pasti vegetariani sono disponibili presso ogni Padiglione. Una scelta di menù vegetariano viene offerta ad ogni pasto.

Allergie: tutti i menù sono preparati con un uso minimo degli alimenti che più comunemente causano allergie, sebbene alcune tracce di questi potrebbero essere presenti. Per prevenire il problema delle allergie, i prodotti contenenti noci sono chiaramente identificabili tramite l'etichetta sulla confezione.

La lista completa degli ingredienti è disponibile presso ogni padiglione che ospita il servizio di ristorazione. Le persone con allergie alimentari dovrebbero avvertire i responsabili del padiglione.

Altri Servizi di Ristorazione

Ad Exhibition Place e a Downsview sono presenti punti vendita autorizzati che offrono una varietà di cibi tipici di diverse culture. Portate con voi del denaro se desiderate provare alcune delle specialità disponibili.

Acqua

Ad ogni pasto vengono fornite bottiglie di acqua da mezzo litro. Potete riempire le bottiglie, gratuitamente, alle stazioni di rifornimento idrico ad Exhibition Place, lungo i sentieri di Pellegrinaggio e a Downsview. E' consigliabile bere molta acqua durante tutto il giorno e approfittare di ogni occasione per riempire le bottiglie. Potete acquistare acqua e altre bibite ad Exhibition Place e a Downsview, e in tutta la città.

PROGRAMMA DEGLI EVENTI

Il programma vi dà la possibilità di fare un'esperienza di Chiesa attraverso gli incontri con il Papa, i ministri della Chiesa e gli altri pellegrini.

I principali incontri di tutti i partecipanti sono:

- **Messa d'Apertura** martedì 23 luglio alle ore 17:00 ad Exhibition Place
- **Cerimonia d'Accoglienza con il Papa** giovedì 25 luglio alle ore 17:00 ad Exhibition Place
- **Via Crucis** venerdì 26 luglio alle ore 19:30, lungo University Avenue
- **Veglia con il Papa** sabato 27 luglio alle ore 19:30 a Downsview
- **Messa Papale** domenica 28 luglio alle ore 9:30 a Downsview

---

Lunedì 22 luglio

Arrivo a Toronto

Arrivo nell'Area Metropolitana di Toronto, sistemazione negli alloggi e incontro con i giovani di Toronto, i quali, insieme alla chiesa locale e all'intera comunità, saranno felici di ospitarvi.

Martedì 23 luglio

Messa di Apertura

Pomeriggio/Sera

- – Sua Eminenza Cardinal Aloysius Ambrozic, Arcivescovo di Toronto, celebra l'Eucaristia ad Exhibition Place alle ore 17:00.
- – Concerto di Apertura ad Exhibition Place, cantano talenti canadesi.
- – Sacramento della Riconciliazione

Mercoledì 24 luglio

Mattina

- Catechesi (momenti di preghiera, discussione e riflessione basati sugli insegnamenti dei vescovi di tutto il mondo)
- Le catechesi sono concluse da una Messa.

Pomeriggio e Sera

- Assistenza Sociale
- Festival della Gioventù, che consiste in attività culturali, spirituali e di intrattenimento
- Sacramento della Riconciliazione

Giovedì 25 luglio

Cerimonia d'Accoglienza con il Papa

Mattino

- Catechesi (vedi mercoledì)

Pomeriggio

- Cerimonia d'Accoglienza con il Papa ad Exhibition Place alle ore 17:00
- Sacramento della Riconciliazione

Sera

- Festival della Gioventù
- Sacramento della Riconciliazione

Venerdì 26 luglio

Via Crucis

Mattino

- Catechesi (come nei giorni precedenti)

Pomeriggio

- Assistenza Sociale
- Festival della Gioventù
- STREETFEST!
- Sacramento della Riconciliazione

Sera

- Via Crucis lungo University Avenue alle ore 19:30

Sabato 27 luglio

Mattino e pomeriggio

- Messa del mattino alle ore 8:00 nelle parrocchie di Toronto
- Pellegrinaggio a piedi verso Downsview
- Concerto d'Accoglienza a Downsview
- Sacramento della Riconciliazione

Veglia con il Papa

Sera

- La Veglia inizia alle ore 19:30 con preghiere, musica, testimonianze ed un messaggio del Papa.
- Il Papa lascia Downsview dopo la Veglia e i pellegrini dormono all'aperto a Downsview.

Domenica 28 luglio

Messa Papale

- Dalle ore 9:30 fino a mezzogiorno il Papa celebra la Messa a Downsview. Questo evento è aperto a tutti i membri del pubblico esterno.

LINGUE DELLA TRADUZIONE SIMULTANEA

Il servizio di traduzione simultanea viene trasmesso via radio per gli eventi seguenti:

- Messa di Apertura, 23 luglio
- Cerimonia d'Accoglienza con il Papa, 25 luglio
- Via Crucis, 26 luglio
- Veglia con il Papa, 27 luglio
- Messa Papale, 28 luglio

Le informazioni contenute in questa tabella sono soggette a cambiamenti

Lingua	Banda di Frequenza FM	Lingua	Banda di Frequenza FM
Inglese	104.9	Francese	103.9
Spagnolo	101.7	Italiano	102.7
Portoghese	99.5	Polacco	91.9
Tedesco	90.7	Arabo	98.7

FESTIVAL DELLA GIOVENTÙ

Il Festival della Gioventù costituisce un momento di unione per i giovani, permettendo loro di esprimere le proprie tradizioni, culture, lingue ed esperienze. Avrà luogo di sera dal 23 luglio al 25 luglio, e di pomeriggio il 24 e il 25 luglio. Gli eventi comprendono:

Performance

Cinquecento performance avranno luogo in 25 palchi, mettendo in scena musica, danza, teatro e cinema.

STREETFEST!

Venerdì 26 luglio, nel pomeriggio, artisti di strada si esibiranno lungo Unversity Avenue.

Preghiera

Nelle chiese di Toronto e in altri luoghi sarà messa in risalto la grande varietà di esperienze di preghiera e lode.

Mostre

Ad Exhibition Place saranno esposte alcune mostre sul tema dell'arte, della cultura, delle vocazioni, dell'assistenza sociale e della giustizia sociale.

Seminari

In diversi luoghi si terranno forum di discussione riguardanti una vasta gamma di argomenti.

Incontri

Presso chiese e parchi ci sarà l'opportunità di incontrarsi e celebrare, sulla base di spiritualità, lingua o etnia comuni.

Caffè

Discussioni informali avranno luogo nei caffè, alcuni dei quali avranno il servizio internet.

Attività Vocazionali

Il Padiglione Vocazione e Servizio ad Exhibition Place offre un posto dove poter riflettere su una potenziale chiamata di Dio. Vi offrirà anche la possibilità di incontrare, parlare e celebrare momenti con altri giovani.

Festival del Cinema

Verrà presentata una selezione di film a tema religioso, inclusa la prima mondiale di un documentario su Madre Teresa di Calcutta.

Immagini di Salvezza

Il Royal Ontario Museum (ROM) sta ospitando una mostra dal titolo *Immagini di Salvezza*, che presenta più di 100 capolavori provenienti dalle collezioni vaticane ed italiane. Il ROM si trova al 100 di Queen's Park, all'incrocio tra Bloor Street

West e Avenue Road, accanto alla stazione "Museum" della metropolitana. L'orario di apertura del ROM dal 21 al 27 luglio è: dalle ore 10:00 alle 21:30. Mostrando il pass otterrete un biglietto d'entrata al prezzo speciale di 5 dollari.

Tempo Libero

Alcuni parchi di Toronto offriranno la possibilità di partecipare a giochi e attività sportive.

Assistenza Sociale

Avrete la possibilità di prendere parte ad alcune attività di assistenza sociale, per lasciare un messaggio di altruismo e per mostrare la nostra fede con i fratelli e le sorelle di tutte le confessioni. I gruppi che si sono iscritti alle attività di assistenza sociale parteciperanno a sessioni di tre ore ciascuna, dalle ore 14:30 alle ore 17:30 di mercoledì 24 luglio e venerdì 26 luglio.

Ci sono tre tipi di attività di assistenza sociale:

– Progetti di assistenza che forniscono un aiuto diretto alle persone

– Discussioni su specifici temi di servizio

– Visite ad organizzazioni di servizio locali

Catechesi

Le catechesi avranno luogo mercoledì 24 luglio, giovedì 25 luglio e venerdì 26 luglio, organizzate per gruppi linguistici, e dislocate in punti diversi. I vescovi di tutto il mondo condurranno tali sessioni mattutine sull'insegnamento della fede cattolica, ed esse includeranno anche la partecipazione ai sacramenti dell'Eucarestia e della Riconciliazione.

Gli argomenti delle catechesi sono:

Mercoledì *Voi Siete il Sale della Terra*

Giovedì *Voi Siete la Luce del Mondo*

Venerdì *Siate Riconciliati con Dio*

Sacramento della Riconciliazione

Ci saranno tre occasioni per accostarsi al Sacramento della Riconciliazione:

- Presso i luoghi delle catechesi, i sacerdoti saranno disponibili di mattina, da mercoledì 24 luglio a venerdì 26 luglio

- Al Parco Duc in Altum, ad est del cancello principale di Exhibition Place, diverse centinaia di sacerdoti saranno disponibili:
  - Martedì 23 luglio dalle ore 14:00 alle ore 16:00 e dalle ore 18:00 alle ore 20:00
  - Mercoledì 24 luglio dalle ore 14:00 alle ore 20:00
  - Giovedì 25 luglio dalle ore 14:00 alle ore 16:00 e dalle ore 18:00 alle ore 20:00
  - Venerdì 26 luglio dalle ore 14:00 alle ore 18:00

- A Downsview, alcuni sacerdoti saranno disponibili sabato 27 luglio dalle ore 14:00 fino all'inizio della Veglia con il Papa.

PUNTO VENDITA UFFICIALE DELLA GMG

Potete acquistare i prodotti ufficiali della GMG in tre posti: nel punto vendita ufficiale della GMG, che si trova al 433 di Yonge Street, vicino alla stazione "College" della metropolitana; ad Exhibition Place e a Downsview, dove sono presenti grandi stand in cui acquistare souvenir, libri, musica e articoli di abbigliamento.

VOLONTARI

- I Volontari saranno presenti ad ogni evento per aiutare voi e gli organizzatori degli eventi. Saranno presenti anche presso gli Info Point dislocati in tutta la città.

- I volontari possono comunicare nelle quattro lingue ufficiali della GMG: inglese, francese, spagnolo e italiano. Non esitate a chiedere aiuto ad un volontario.

- I volontari portano una maglietta blu con il logo che vedete qui sotto.

BÉNÉVOLE
WYD2002JMJ
VOLUNTEER

RISPETTO DELL'AMBIENTE

- Saranno disponibili scatole di cartone appositamente segnalate per la raccolta differenziata di bottiglie, lattine e materiale cartaceo, quale giornali, riviste, involucri alimentari puliti. Grandi buste di carta sono invece disponibili per l'eliminazione di rifiuti deperibili (resti di alimenti). Siete pregati di seguire le istruzioni nelle scatole e nelle buste e di riciclare il più possibile.

- A Downsview ci sarà bisogno del vostro aiuto per spostare i contenitori pieni della raccolta differenziata verso la strada, perché vengano svuotati, e poi per riportarli vuoti nella vostra area.

- Non appena ne avete l'occasione, raccogliete i rifiuti che trovate in giro e gettateli negli appositi contenitori.

- Nella maggior parte delle strade principali sono disponibili bidoni dei rifiuti e contenitori per la raccolta differenziata.

TELEFONI

- Una chiamata locale da un telefono pubblico costa 25 centesimi ($0,25). I numeri di telefono canadesi hanno un minimo di sette cifre, mentre in alcune città più grandi, come Toronto e l'area circostante, è necessario aggiungere un prefisso di tre cifre anche per le chiamate locali. I prefissi per Toronto sono 416 e 647. Per l'Area Metropolitana di Toronto i prefissi sono 905 e 289.

- Per le chiamate interurbane, sia all'interno del Canada che dal Canada per gli Stati Uniti, è necessario digitare 1 + prefisso + numero locale. Per le chiamate verso gli altri paesi è necessario comporre lo 011 + prefisso del paese + prefisso della città + numero locale. Per le chiamate tramite operatore: chiamate dirette, con schede telefoniche (Calling Card), addebitate ad una terza persona e a carico, comporre lo 01 + prefisso del paese + prefisso della città + numero locale. La lista dei prefissi internazionali si trova nella sezione iniziale dell'elenco del telefono.

- E' possibile acquistare schede telefoniche ufficiali della GMG da 10 e 20 dollari presso i punti iscrizione, a Downsview e ad Exhibition Place. Queste schede, prodotte in una serie da 12, da collezionare, sono valide per chiamate in tutto il mondo dal Canada e dagli USA.

- In molti posti è anche possibile affittare telefoni cellulari.

ACCESSO AD INTERNET

- Le 98 sezioni della Toronto Public Libraries (TPL – Biblioteche Pubbliche di Toronto) offrono accesso gratuito ad internet, con connessione ad alta velocità.

- La sede principale della TPL, la Toronto Reference Library (789 Yonge Street, un isolato a nord di Bloor Street), contiene più di 100 postazioni Internet e offre più di 100 testate giornalistiche provenienti da tutto il mondo.

- Per maggiori informazioni, chiamate la TPL Answerline al (416) 393-7131.
- L'accesso ad Internet è disponibile anche presso alcuni dei caffè del Festival della Gioventù.

ELETTRICITÀ

Il Canada utilizza il sistema di voltaggio a 110 volt, al contrario dell'Europa e di molti altri paesi, che usano il sistema a 220 – 240 volt.

DENARO E TASSE

- La valuta Canadese è espressa in dollari e centesimi. Il dollaro americano offre un cambio favorevole
- Per ottenere il miglior tasso di cambio possibile, cambiate il denaro presso istituti finanziari riconosciuti, quali banche, società di credito o cambio valuta.
- Le monete canadesi da uno e due dollari sono comunemente chiamate rispettivamente *loonie* e *toonie*. Ogni taglio di moneta cartacea è contraddistinto da un diverso colore. Molti esercizi commerciali non accettano banconote da 50 dollari o più.

Imposte sul Valore Aggiunto

Il Goods and Services Tax (GST – Tassa sui Beni e Servizi) è una imposta federale del 7 percento applicata sulla maggior parte dei beni e servizi. Come parte della provincia dell'Ontario, la città di Toronto impone anche una imposta provinciale sul valore aggiunto (PST), pari all' 8 percento, applicata alla maggior parte delle merci in vendita.

Rimborsi Tasse per Turisti

- I visitatori non residenti in Canada hanno diritto al rimborso della GST sull'acquisto di certi beni che intendono portare fuori del Canada, e anche sulle spese alberghiere, limitatamente a brevi periodi.

- Se desiderate richiedere il rimborso della GST, conservate le ricevute degli acquisti e degli hotel. E' possibile ottenere una copia della Richiesta di Rimborso delle Tasse per Turisti (*Tax Refund Application for Visitors*) presso qualsiasi dogana canadese oppure presso la maggior parte dei centri di informazione turistica, duty-free shop, centri commerciali, e alcuni hotel.

- Tali moduli di richiesta sono disponibili anche presso molti Info Point a Downsview ed Exhibition Place. Per un veloce svolgimento della pratica, portate le ricevute di acquisto e un documento che dimostri che non siete residenti in Canada.

Carte di Credito/Bancomat

- Le più diffuse carte di credito, come Visa, MasterCard, American Express e Diners Club sono accettate ovunque. Nel rendiconto mensile, il vostro istituto finanziario provvederà a convertire automaticamente i dollari canadesi nella valuta del vostro paese.

- La maggior parte dei bancomat canadesi (ABM) accettano le vostre carte di credito nei sistemi Bancomat, Cirrus e Plus. Oltre che nelle banche, i bancomat si trovano negli aeroporti, in alcuni palazzi governativi e in molti negozi.

- In caso di perdita della carta di credito, contattate immediatamente il vostro istituto finanziario e denunciate lo smarrimento alla polizia.

SERVIZI POSTALI

- I francobolli si trovano in vendita, oltre che negli uffici postali canadesi, anche in molte farmacie, empori e alimentari.

- Lettere e cartoline si spediscono imbucandole nelle cassette della posta, situate nei pressi degli incroci principali.

- Per servizi postali diversi, quali ad esempio la spedizione di un pacco o di una raccomandata, è necessario rivolgersi agli uffici postali. Questi si trovano all'interno di determinati esercizi commerciali, come farmacie, empori, ed altri negozi. I negozi che ospitano al loro interno un ufficio postale, hanno affisso all'esterno, o nella vetrina, il logo delle Poste Canadesi (vedi sotto).

- Il costo per spedire lettere standard, comprese le cartoline, è di 48 centesimi per il Canada, 65 centesimi per gli Stati Uniti e 1,25 dollari per tutti gli altri paesi.

YOUTH FESTIVAL SCHEDULE

HORAIRE DU FESTIVAL DE LA JEUNESSE

CRONOGRAMA DEL FESTIVAL JUVENIL

PROGRAMMA DEL FESTIVAL DELLA GIOVENTÙ

YOUTH FESTIVAL SYMBOLS
SYMBOLES DU FESTIVAL DE LA JEUNESSE
SÍMBOLOS DEL FESTIVAL JUVENIL
SIMBOLI DEL FESTIVAL DELLA GIOVENTÙ

Café Café Café Caffé			Internet Internet Internet Internet
Dance Danse Danzas Danza			Music Musique Música Musica
Exhibits Expositions Exposiciones Mostre			Prayer Prière Oración Preghiera
Film Film Películas Cinema			Seminar Séminaire Seminario Seminari
Gathering Rassemblement Encuentro Incontri			Theatre Théâtre Teatro Teatro

This schedule is subject to change. Cet horaire est sujet à changement.
Este cronograma está sujeto a cambios. Questo programma è soggetto a cambiamenti

YOUTH FESTIVAL SCHEDULE

Start	End		Location	Type of Event

Tuesday – 7/23/02

9:00	12:00	**Syro-Malabar Catholic Diocese of Chicago** (International) *Malayalee/Kerala Youth Gathering*	Holy Cross Parish	
10:00	13:00	**Arbeitsstelle für Jugendseelsorge** (Germany) *German Youth Gathering: Scout Festival*	Exhibition Place NTC – Hall C	
10:00	13:00	**Australian Delegation** (Australia) *Australian World Youth Day Gathering*	Exhibition Place Queen Elizabeth Hall	
10:00	13:00	**Focolare** (International) *Interfaith dialogue to build the universal family / Dialogue interreligieux pour construire une famille universelle*	St. Patrick's Parish	
10:00	13:00	**Région apostolique Île de France** (France) *Recontre des jeunes de la la région apostolique île de France*	Exhibition Place Automotive Building – Ground Floor	
10:00	11:30	**Taizé Community/Communauté de Taizé** (France) *Taizé Prayer/Prière de Taizé*	St. Paul's Parish	
10:00	13:00	**Youth to Youth Catholic Evangelization** (USA) *Prayer with Music and Scripture*	Holy Name Parish	
12:00	15:00	**Austrian Bishops Conference WYD Committee** (Austria) *Austrian Youth Gathering: Österreichertreffen*	St. Helen's Parish	
12:00	12:30	**Lechowia Polish Canadian Folk Dance Company** (Canada)	Ontario Place Festival Stage	
12:00	12:45	**Sheep** (Canada) *Alternative Praise Concert featuring Sheep*	Exhibition Place Marilyn Bell Park-East	
12:00	17:10	**St. Michael's Cathedral** (Canada) *Adoration*	St. Michael's Cathedral	
12:00	13:30	**Taizé Community/Communauté de Taizé** (France) *Taizé Prayer/Prière de Taizé*	St. Paul's Parish	
12:00	14:00	**WORLD STAGE** (International) *Kool Matope, Grupo Rukanas, Nunavut Performers, M. Kante Moussa Pathe, Dnipro Ukranian Dance Ensemble*	Metro Square	

Start	End		Location	Type of Event
Tuesday – 7/23/02				
12:15	13:00	**Sheldon Casavant** (Canada) *The Magic of Sheldon*	Ontario Place Island Club	
12:30	13:15	**Encounter** (Australia)	Exhibition Place Bandshell	
12:30	13:15	**Gospel Myriam** (Canada)	Mel Lastman Square	
13:00	14:00	**Conjunto Danzante de Tijeras - Ayacucho** (Peru)	Exhibition Place Marilyn Bell Park – West	
13:00	14:00	**Emmanuel Community** (International) *Jacob's Well*	Exhibition Place Bandshell Café	
13:00	15:00	**Hallain Paluku & Alain Mata** (Congo) *Cartoonists/Dessinateur de Bande*	Exhibition Place Café Soleil	
13:00	13:45	**Irenne Coronado** (Guatemala)	Ontario Place Festival Stage	
13:00	15:00	**Madonna House** (Canada) *A Woman in Love*	Newman Centre Catholic Mission	
13:00	13:30	**PAX ROMANA** (Ghana)	Exhibition Place Main Stage	
13:15	15:15	**MAKE NOISE! Young Voices sing to our Awesome God!** (International) *Circle of Friends, Leah Cogan, Brianna Dyer, Breanne Arrigo, Cristina Plancher, Kelly Pease*	Exhibition Place Marilyn Bell Park – East	
13:30	14:15	**Ceili Rain** (USA)	Ontario Place Island Club	
13:30	14:00	**Steve Angrisano & Tony Melendez** (USA)	Exhibition Place Main Stage	
13:45	14:30	**Kerygma Fuego Nuevo** (Mexico)	Mel Lastman Square	
13:45	14:30	**TERI V** (Canada) *Teri Vissani*	Exhibition Place Bandshell	
14:00	15:30	**Groupe des jeunes de lumière** (Congo)	Exhibition Place Automotive Building – Ground Floor	
14:00	14:30	**Susan Hookong-Taylor** (Canada)	Exhibition Place Main Stage	
14:15	15:00	**Pinstripe Project** (Canada)	Ontario Place Festival Stage	
14:30	15:15	**St. Michael's Choir School** (Canada)	Metro Square	

YOUTH FESTIVAL SCHEDULE

Start	End		Location	Type of Event

Tuesday – 7/23/02

Start	End		Location	Type of Event
14:45	15:30	**Logan Alexis Round Dance Singers** (Canada) *(Canadian Aboriginal Cultural Performer)*	Ontario Place Island Club	🎵
15:00	15:30	**Don Mimmo** (Italy)	Exhibition Place Bandshell	🎵
15:00	15:45	**Strait Shooters** (Canada)	Mel Lastman Square	🎵
19:00	19:30	**Denis Grady** (Canada)	Exhibition Place Coliseum-Industry (Hall G)	🎵
19:00	22:00	**Life Teen, Inc.** (USA) *We Can Change the World: Being a Light of Christ Today*	Exhibition Place NTC – (Hall A)	🧍
19:00	20:00	**Who Do You Say I Am?** (USA)	Exhibition Place Bandshell	🎵
19:00	22:00	**Youth Arise International** (Canada) *Praise & Worship*	Exhibition Place Automotive Building – Ground Floor	🧍
19:30	20:15	**Kairos** (Poland)	Exhibition Place Queen Elizabeth Hall	🩰
19:45	20:30	**Wheels in Motion Dance Co.** (USA) *Celebration of Youth*	Exhibiton Place Coliseum-Arena	🩰
20:00	21:00	**Ana Pozas** (Spain)	St. Peter's Parish	🎵
20:00	22:00	**CAP Jeunesse** (Canada)	Exhibition Place NTC – (Hall C)	🎭
20:00	22:00	**Dave Rodney – Mount Everest Two-Time Summiteer** (Canada) *Sacred Spaces – Climbing Physical & Spiritual Mountains*	Exhibition Place NTC – S103 (Hall A)	🧗
20:00	20:45	**Dornbusch Band** (Germany) *Live in Concert*	Ontario Place Festival Stage	🎵
20:00	20:45	**Duc In Altum** (Peru) *Luz en las Tinieblas*	Exhibition Place Marilyn Bell Park-East	🎭
20:00	23:00	**Eastern Catholic Churches (Ss. Peter & Paul Melkite Catholic Church – Ottawa)** (International) *Eastern Catholic Encounter*	St. Nicholas Ukrainian Catholic	🕺
20:00	22:00	**Gino Fillion** (Canada) *Le Maître, Notre Ami*	Exhibition Place Coliseum-Industry (Hall G)	🎵

Start	End		Location	Type of Event
Tuesday – 7/23/02				
20:00	23:00	**Jeunes des Sources - Aumônerie du Sundgau** (France) *Veillée "Passeurs de lumière"*	Newman Centre Catholic Mission	
20:00	22:00	**NAHUI OLLIN** (Mexico) *El milagro del Tepeyac*	Exhibition Place Queen Elizabeth Theatre	
20:00	20:45	**Nunavut Performers** (Canada)	Ontario Place Island Club	
20:00	21:00	**Scarecrow & Tinmen** (USA)	Ontario Place Molson Amphitheatre	
20:00	21:00	**Sean Forrest** (USA)	Exhibition Place Dufferin Bandstand	
20:00	20:45	**Shalom** (USA)	Mel Lastman Square	
20:00	22:00	**Welcome Concert** (Canada)	Exhibition Place Main Stage	
20:15	21:00	**Nana Angarita** (Colombia)	Nathan Phillips Square	
20:15	21:00	**Spice Island Youthquake** (Grenada)	Metro Square	
20:30	23:00	**Communauté du Chemin Neuf** (France) *Fête pour Dieu*	St. Patrick's Parish	
20:30	22:00	**Comunidade Católica Shalom** (Brazil) *Coração do Homem*	Exhibition Place Queen Elizabeth Hall	
20:30	22:00	**Critical Mass John 6:35,51** (Canada) *Critical Mass and Friends*	Exhibition Place Bandshell	
20:30	22:00	**Taizé Community/Communauté de Taizé** (France) *Taizé Prayer/Prière de Taizé*	St. Paul's Parish	
21:00	23:00	**Jerusalem** (Sweden)	Ontario Place Molson Amphitheatre	
21:00	23:00	**La Francophonie, Un Message Universel (F.M.U.)** (Canada) *Concert et Messe*	Our Lady of the Assumption	
21:00	23:00	**Piarist Fathers** (USA) *Evening Prayer and Piarist Prayer (Crown of Twelve Stars)*	Santa Cruz Parish	
21:00	22:30	**Servizio Nazionale Pastorale Giovanile Della C.E.I.** (Italy) *Via Lucis*	St. Helen's Parish	

Start	End		Location	Type of Event

Tuesday – 7/23/02

Start	End		Location	Type of Event
21:00	22:00	**Takillakta** (Peru)	Exhibition Place Dufferin Bandstand	
21:00	23:00	**Weltjugendtags-Team** (Germany) *International Ecumenical Rosary for Peace*	Our Lady of Mount Carmel Parish	
21:15	22:15	**Crispin** (USA)	Ontario Place Festival Stage	
21:15	22:00	**In Ipsa** (Canada) *Famille Marie-Jeunesse*	Ontario Place Island Club	
21:15	22:00	**Inés De Viaud** (El Salvador)	St. Peter's Parish	
21:15	22:00	**Starfield** (Canada)	Ontario Place Island Club	
21:15	22:00	**William Pak – True Love Waits** (French Polynesia) *True Love Waits*	Exhibition Place Marilyn Bell Park-East	
21:30	22:15	**Alfa y Omega** (Uruguay)	Nathan Phillips Square	
21:30	23:30	**Equilibrio Precario Company** (Chile) *Mitos de la Muerte y otros Mitos*	St. Michael's College Alumni Hall	
21:30	22:15	**Saruel Music** (Poland)	Metro Square	

Wednesday – 7/24/02

Start	End		Location	Type of Event
12:00	12:45	**Angelica Di Castro** (Canada)	Metro Square	
12:00	12:45	**David A. Vogel & Band** (USA)	Trinity Bellwoods Park	
12:00	12:45	**Irenne Coronado** (Guatemala)	Exhibiton Place Marilyn Bell Park-East	
12:00	12:30	**Kelly Pease** (USA)	Ontario Place Festival Stage	
12:00	17:10	**St. Michael's Cathedral** (Canada) *Adoration*	St. Michael's Cathedral	
12:15	13:00	**dAYZ wAGE** (Canada)	Ontario Place Island Club	
12:15	13:00	**Robert Ekonomou** (USA)	Exhibition Place Bandshell	
12:30	13:15	**Julie Lafontaine** (Canada)	Mel Lastman Square	

Start	End		Location	Type of Event
Wednesday – 7/24/02				
13:00	13:45	**Bangladesher Dhol** (Bangladesh) *The Drums of Bangladesh*	Ontario Place Festival Stage	
13:00	14:00	**Bruce Deaton** (USA)	Exhibition Place Dufferin Bandstand	
13:00	13:45	**Fr. Liam Lawton** (Ireland)	Metro Square	
13:00	13:45	**Gospel Rain** (Poland)	Exhibition Place Main Stage	
13:00	15:00	**Hallain Paluku & Alain Mata** (Congo) *Cartoonists/Dessinateur de Bande*	Exhibition Place Café Soleil	
13:00	20:00	**Konferencja Episkopatu Polski** (Poland) *Dzien Polski - Polish Youth Festival*	Centennial Park Etobicoke	
13:00	15:00	**Productions du Grand Large** (France) *Kateri*	Exhibition Place Medieval Times Arena	
13:00	18:00	**Vietnamese Committee for Vietnamese in Diaspora** (International) *Vietnamese Gathering*	Riverdale Park	
13:15	14:00	**Jésed** (Mexico) *St.Therese y Jésed en concierto*	Trinity Bellwoods Park	
13:15	14:00	**Royal Canadian Mounted Police** (Canada) *Musical Ride*	Exhibition Place Marilyn Bell Park-East	
13:30	14:15	**Bernie Choiniere** (USA)	Ontario Place Island Club	
13:30	14:15	**Chants et Danses de Polynésie** (Tahiti)	Exhibition Place Bandshell	
13:30	15:30	**Gospel Myriam** (Canada)	Exhibition Place Queen Elizabeth Theatre	
13:45	14:30	**Marlene O'Neill** (Canada)	Mel Lastman Square	
14:00	15:00	**Anthony DeBlois** (USA)	Newman Centre Catholic Mission	
14:00	18:00	**Canadian Catholic Campus Ministry** (Canada) *University students meeting with Jean Vanier*	Exhibition Place Coliseum-Arena	
4:00	14:45	**Dawn Kinsman** (USA)	Exhibition Place NTC – Hall C	

YOUTH FESTIVAL SCHEDULE

Start	End		Location	Type of Event
Wednesday – 7/24/02				
14:00	14:30	**Don Mimmo** (Italy)	Exhibition Place Automotive Building – Ground Floor	
14:00	14:45	**Dornbusch Band** (Germany) *Live in Concert*	Exhibition Place Marilyn Bell Park-East	
14:00	15:00	**Eastern Catholic Churches** (Canada) *Redemptorist Martyrs from Ukraine*	Exhibition Place NTC – S107 (Hall B)	
14:00	17:00	**Health Care Professionals/ Educators** (Canada) *Our Health, Our Technology, and Our God: An Interactive Forum on Health Care*	St. Michael's College Fr. Madden Hall	
14:00	18:00	**International Movement for Catholic Agricultural & Rural Youth** (Inernational) *Food Security*	St. Michael's College Sam Sorbara Hall	
14:00	17:00	**Jesus Youth** (India) *In service of the Church*	Holy Cross Parish	
14:00	17:00	**Jeunesse Étudiante Catholique Inc.** (Canada) *Innocent ou coupable?*	Exhibition Place NTC – S103 (Hall A)	
14:00	22:00	**Juventud Mariana Vincenciana** (International) *Young People in the Spirit of St. Vincent de Paul*	Our Lady of the Miraculous Medal	
14:00	15:00	**Louis & Joseph Remlin** (USA) *International Rosary*	Santa Cruz Parish	
14:00	16:00	**Lynn Geyer & John Stufano / ColorBlindMusic Ministries** (USA) *Journey to Forgiveness: The Way of the Cross*	Our Lady of Mount Carmel Parish	
14:00	16:00	**Novalis Publications** (Canada) *Seminar for Young Writers*	Exhibition Place NTC – S105 (Hall A)	
14:00	14:45	**PAX ROMANA** (Ghana)	Exhibition Place NTC – Hall A	
14:00	14:45	**Sara Torres** (Nicaragua)	Exhibition Place Coliseum-Industry (Hall G)	
14:00	16:00	**Sr. Priscilla Solomon** CSJ (Canada) *Rediscovering, Recognizing and Celebrating the Spiritual Heritage of Canada's Aboriginal Peoples*	St. Ann's Parish	
14:00	15:00	**Susan Bailey** (USA)	Exhibition Place Dufferin Bandstand	

Start	End		Location	Type of Event

Wednesday – 7/24/02

Start	End		Location	Type of Event
14:00	15:30	**Taizé Community/Communauté de Taizé** (France) *Taizé Prayer/Prière de Taizé*	St. Paul's Parish	
14:00	18:00	**World Youth Alliance** (International) *The Dignity of the Human Person*	Exhibition Place Queen Elizabeth Hall	
14:00	16:30	**WYD 2002 Design Department** (Canada) *The Living Tradition: A Discussion Group and Forum on Sacred Art and Architecture*	Royal Ontario Museum Theatre	
14:15	15:00	**Matt Maher with Danielle Rose** (Canada, USA)	Ontario Place Festival Stage	
14:15	15:00	**Migueli** (Spain)	Exhibition Place Main Stage	
14:15	15:00	**Spirit Blazers** (Canada)	Metro Square	
14:30	15:15	**Shalom** (USA)	Trinity Bellwoods Park	
14:30	18:00	**Youth to Youth Catholic Evangelization** (USA) *Prayer with Music and Scripture*	Holy Name Parish	
14:45	15:30	**Jerry Aull** (USA) *Jerry Aull Music*	Ontario Place Island Club	
14:45	15:30	**Sarah Hart** (USA)	Exhibition Place Bandshell	
15:00	17:30	**Canadian Catholic Organization for Development and Peace** (Canada) *Josanthony Joseph (India), Mohau Pheko (South Africa): Building Communities of Justice*	Exhibition Place NTC – Hall A	
15:00	16:00	**Eastern Catholic Churches** (Canada) *The Dialogue of Love: Catholic-Orthodox Ecumenism*	Exhibition Place NTC – S107 (Hall B)	
15:00	18:00	**Focolare** (Inernational) *Interfaith dialogue to build the universal family / Dialogue interreligieux pour construire une famille universelle /*	St. Patrick's Parish	
15:00	17:30	**Habitat for Humanity** (Canada) *Millard Fuller*	Exhibition Place Automotive Building – Ground Floor	
15:00	16:00	**Jon Callegher** (Canada) *Renew Your Faith*	Santa Cruz Parish	

Start	End		Location	Type of Event
Wednesday – 7/24/02				
15:00	18:00	**Novalis Publications** (Canada) *Forum pour les jeunes écrivains*	Exhibition Place NTC – S102 (Hall A)	
15:00	21:00	**Salesian Youth Movement / Mouvement Jeunesse Salésienne du Canada** (Canada) *International Salesian Youth Rally / Rallye International Salésien*	Msgr. Percy Secondary School	
15:00	15:45	**Spirit in Motion** (Canada)	Mel Lastman Square	
15:00	16:00	**St. Michael's Choir School** (Canada)	St. Michael's Cathedral	
15:00	17:30	**United States Conference of Catholic Bishops** (USA) *Prayer for Vocations: Come, Follow Me*	St. Helen's Parish	
15:15	16:00	**Eric J Sova Ministry** (USA)	Exhibition Place Marilyn Bell Park-East	
15:15	16:00	**Judy Fleming** (Canada)	Exhibition Place Coliseum-Industry (Hall G)	
15:30	17:00	**Hermana Glenda** (Spain)	St. Peter's Parish	
15:30	16:15	**Jordan Zed** (Canada)	Metro Square	
15:30	16:15	**Padre Zeca** (Brazil)	Exhibition Place Main Stage	
15:30	16:15	**TERI V** (Canada) *Teri Vissani*	Ontario Place Festival Stage	
15:30	17:00	**TrypTych Productions** (Canada) *Magnifichant*	Newman Centre Catholic Mission	
15:45	16:30	**Unis-Sons de fondacio – Chrétiens pour le monde** (France) *Unis-Sons*	Trinity Bellwoods Park	
16:00	18:00	**Daily Mass** (Canada) *Televised Mass*	St. Michael's Cathedral	
16:00	17:00	**Emmanuel Community** (International) *Jacob's Well*	Exhibition Place Bandshell Café	
16:00	17:30	**Jesuits** (Canada) *Lives of the Martyrs*	Exhibition Place Queen Elizabeth Theatre	
16:00	16:45	**Steve Angrisano** (USA)	Exhibition Place Bandshell	

Start	End		Location	Type of Event

Wednesday – 7/24/02

Start	End		Location	Type of Event
16:00	17:30	**Taizé Community/Communauté de Taizé** (France) *Taizé Prayer/Prière de Taizé*	St. Paul's Parish	
16:00	16:45	**Tony Melendez** (USA)	Ontario Place Island Club	
16:00	16:45	**Vietnamese Lasallian Youth** (USA) *Frère Phong & Friends*	Nathan Phillips Square	
16:15	17:00	**Scarecrow & Tinmen** (USA)	Mel Lastman Square	
16:30	17:15	**Greg Magirescu** (Canada)	Exhibition Place Coliseum-Industry (Hall G)	
16:30	17:30	**Lynn Cooper** (USA)	Exhibition Place Dufferin Bandstand	
16:30	18:00	**Madonna House** (Canada) *A Woman in Love*	St. Michael's College Alumni Hall	
16:30	17:15	**Mark Mallet** (Canada)	Exhibition Place Marilyn Bell Park-East	
16:30	17:00	**The Resurrection Dance Theatre of Haiti** (Haiti) *Wings of Hope*	Our Lady of Mount Carmel Parish	
16:45	17:30	**100 voix du 7' 8** (France)	Metro Square	
16:45	17:30	**Dom Dominque Minier/Splendor** (Canada)	Exhibition Place Main Stage	
16:45	17:30	**Kelita** (Canada)	Metro Square	
16:45	17:30	**Sean Forrest** (USA)	Ontario Place Festival Stage	
17:00	19:00	**Dave Rodney – Mount Everest Two-Time Summiteer** (Canada) *Sports & Spirituality*	Exhibition Place NTC - S103 (Hall A)	
17:00	19:00	**Faith and Values Media** (USA) *Jeff Kevins, Barbara Nicolosi, Ed Murray: Faith & Values in Television & Film Productions*	Exhibition Place NTC - S107 (Hall B)	
17:00	18:30	**Jeunes du Diocèse de Franceville** (Gabon) *L' Anti-sorcier et la Science (danses traditionnelles du GABON)*	Trinity Bellwoods Park	
17:00	19:00	**Productions du Grand Large** (France) *Kateri*	Exhibition Place Medieval Times Arena	

YOUTH FESTIVAL SCHEDULE

Start	End		Location	Type of Event
Wednesday – 7/24/02				
17:15	18:00	**Ana Pozas** (Spain)	Ontario Place Island Club	
17:15	18:00	**OCP** (International) *Chung Loi Tan Tung*	Exhibition Place Bandshell	
17:15	18:00	**Wheels in Motion Dance Co.** (USA) *Celebration of Youth*	Nathan Phillips Square	
17:30	18:30	**Alas del Alma** (Argentina)	St. Peter's Parish	
17:30	18:30	**Group Gabonais** (Gabon) *Chants et danses*	Our Lady of the Assumption	
17:30	18:15	**Sheep** (Canada) *Alternative Praise Concert featuring Sheep*	Mel Lastman Square	
17:45	18:30	**Kerygma Fuego Nuevo** (Mexico)	Exhibition Place Marilyn Bell Park-East	
17:45	18:30	**Remnant** (USA)	Exhibition Place Coliseum-Industry (Hall G)	
17:45	18:30	**Tohono O'odham Nation – World Youth Day Circle** (USA)	Exhibition Place Automotive Building – Ground Floor	
18:00	19:00	**Bobby Fischer** (USA)	Exhibition Place Dufferin Bandstand	
18:00	22:00	**Conferenza Episcopale Italiana (CEI)** (Italy) *ITALYANI*	Ontario Place Molson Amphitheatre	
18:00	20:00	**Denis Grady** (Canada)	St. Bonaventure Parish	
18:00	21:00	**Eastern Catholic Churches** (Canada) *Malankara Prayer Experience*	Holy Cross Parish	
18:00	23:00	**FABC Office of Laity** (Asia) *Asian Youth Gathering – Shine on...Asia!*	Exhibition Place NTC – Hall C	
18:00	19:30	**Fraternités Monastiques de Jérusalem Paris** (France) *Vêpres pour la paix*	Our Lady of Lebanon Church	
18:00	18:45	**Gino Fillion** (Canada) *Gino Fillion et ses Amis*	Metro Square	
18:00	18:45	**Greg Walton** (USA)	Ontario Place Festival Stage	
18:00	18:45	**Heruvymy Ukrainian Female Quartet** (Canada)	St. Nicholas Ukrainian Catholic	

Start	End		Location	Type of Event
Wednesday – 7/24/02				
18:00	18:45	**Jubilee Singers** (Canada)	St. Helen's Parish	
18:00	18:45	**Mark Masri** (Canada)	Exhibition Place Main Stage	
18:00	19:00	**Nick Alexander** (USA)	Holy Name Parish	
18:00	21:00	**Scalabrini Fathers** (Canada) *Struggles of Migrants*	St. Anthony's Parish	
18:00	19:30	**Taizé Community/Communauté de Taizé** (France) *Taizé Prayer/Prière de Taizé*	St. Paul's Parish	
18:30	19:15	**Aaron Thompson** (USA) *Aaron Thompson and Soul Pigeon*	Ontario Place Island Club	
18:30	19:30	**Angelo Paquette** (Canada)	Exhibition Place Coliseum-Arena	
18:30	19:15	**Associação Juvenil João Paulo II** (Cabo Verde) *Cabo Verde, seca e escravatura*	Nathan Phillips Square	
18:30	20:00	**Duc In Altum** (Peru) *Peregrinos de Esperanza*	St. Michael's College Alumni Hall	
18:30	19:30	**EnREDados** (Latin America) *Migueli, Martin Valverde, Ziza y Daniel Poli*	Exhibition Place Bandshell	
18:30	22:00	**Vicaría Pastoral Universitaria-Arzobispado de Santiago de Chile** (Chile) *Chilean Gathering*	Riverdale Park	
18:45	20:00	**Ceili Rain** (USA)	Mel Lastman Square	
18:45	19:30	**Logan Alexis Round Dance Singers** (Canada) *(Canadian Aboriginal Cultural Performer)*	Exhibition Place Queen Elizabeth Hall	
18:45	19:30	**Semilla Musical** (Columbia)	Exhibition Place NTC - Hall A	
19:00	22:00	**Catholic Association of Musicians** (USA) *CAM Stage*	Exhibition Place Marilyn Bell Park-East	
19:00	21:00	**Catholic Philosophers & Artists** (Canada) *Philosophy and the Arts as Spiritual Exercises*	St. Michael's College Fr. Madden Hall	
19:00	19:45	**Comunidade Católica Shalom** (Brazil) *Uma esperança de paz*	Exhibition Place Coliseum-Industry (Hall G)	

YOUTH FESTIVAL SCHEDULE

Start	End		Location	Type of Event
Wednesday – 7/24/02				
19:00	22:00	**Congregation of Notre Dame** (Canada) *Café Marguerite*	Notre Dame Secondary School	☕
19:00	22:00	**Dominica (Diocese of Roseau)** (Dominica) *Dominica – Culture, Praise and Song*	Santa Cruz Parish	🧎
19:00	20:00	**Eastern Catholic Churches** (USA) *Iconography*	St. Nicholas Ukrainian Catholic	👥
19:00	20:00	**Francesca Ancarola** (Chile)	St. Peter's Parish	🎵
19:00	21:30	**Groupe Culturel et Folklorique Yaka-lunda** (Congo) *Jeunesse du monde catholique-Maloko madibundu dia catholica*	Our Lady of the Assumption	🎵
19:00	21:00	**International Catholic Conference of Scouting** (International) *Scouts Gathering: Catholic Scouts let their Light Shine*	Exhibition Place Dufferin Bandstand	🧑‍🤝‍🧑
19:00	19:45	**Lviv Theological Academy Choir** (Ukraine) *"Stritennia"*	Trinity Bellwoods Park	🎵
19:00	22:00	**Petrie Digital Media L.L.C.** (Canada) *Mother Teresa: The Legacy – World Premiere*	Exhibition Place Queen Elizabeth Theatre	🎬
19:15	20:00	**Chór Akademicki Uniwersytetu im. Adama Mickiewicza Poznaniu** (Poland)	Metro Square	🎵
19:15	20:00	**Decade** (Canada)	Ontario Place Festival Stage	🎵
19:15	20:00	**His Majesty's Musicians** (USA)	Exhibition Place Automotive Building – Ground Floor	🎵
19:15	20:00	**The Rex Band** (India) *The Rex Band Live*	Exhibition Place Main Stage	🎵
19:15	20:00	**Tim Balfe** (England) *Tim Balfe in Concert – "God is not the thief of happiness"*	St. Helen's Parish	🎵
19:30	22:00	**Communauté du Chemin Neuf** (France) *Fête pour Dieu*	St. Patrick's Parish	🧎
19:30	22:00	**United States Conference of Catholic Bishops** (USA) *Prayer for Vocations: Come, Follow Me*	Holy Name Parish	🧎
19:45	20:30	**Alonso Sanabria** (Costa Rica)	Ontario Place Island Club	🎵

Start	End		Location	Type of Event

Wednesday – 7/24/02

Start	End	Event	Location	Type
19:45	20:30	**Communauté du Monastère Invisible** (Lebanon) *Ouvre Ton Cœur à la Lumière du Christ*	Nathan Phillips Square	
19:45	20:30	**Jerusalem** (Sweden)	Nathan Phillips Square	
20:00	20:45	**Afro Gospel Chor Paderborn** (Germany)	Exhibition Place Bandshell	
20:00	22:00	**Comunidade Católica Shalom** (Brazil) *Coração do Homem*	Exhibition Place Queen Elizabeth Hall	
20:00	20:45	**In Ipsa** (Canada) *Famille Marie-Jeunesse*	Exhibition Place Coliseum-Arena	
20:00	22:00	**Irene Tomaszewski** (Canada) *I Am First a Human Being*	Newman Centre Catholic Mission	
20:00	20:45	**La Troupe Folklorique des Chevaliers** (Canada)	Our Lady of Lebanon	
20:00	22:00	**Sal Solo** (USA) *21st Century Evang-A Ganza*	Exhibition Place NTC - Hall A	
20:15	21:00	**Capstone** (Canada)	Exhibition Place Coliseum-Industry (Hall G)	
20:30	21:15	**BDKJ – München und freising** (Germany) *Folk Dances*	Exhibition Place Automotive Building – Ground Floor	
20:30	22:00	**Crispin** (USA)	Mel Lastman Square	
20:30	22:00	**Eastern Catholic Churches** (Canada) *Byzantine Vespers*	Trinity Bellwoods Park	
20:30	22:30	**Ge'la** (Mexico) *Se Llamaba Gabriela*	St. Michael's College Alumni Hall	
20:30	21:30	**Nana Angarita** (Colombia)	Ontario Place Festival Stage	
20:30	22:00	**OCP** (International) *WYD 2002 JMJ CD Live!*	Exhibition Place Main Stage	
20:30	22:00	**Taizé Community/Communauté de Taizé** (France) *Taizé Prayer/Prière de Taizé*	St. Paul's Parish	
20:30	21:15	**Tomek Kamiński** (Poland)	Metro Square	
20:30	22:00	**Tony Melendez** (USA)	Exhibition Place Main Stage	

YOUTH FESTIVAL SCHEDULE

Start	End		Location	Type of Event
Wednesday – 7/24/02				
21:00	22:00	**Fr. Stan Fortuna** (USA)	Exhibition Place Bandshell	🎵
21:00	22:30	**Leahy** (Canada)	Nathan Phillips Square	🎵
21:00	21:45	**The Love Movement** (Trinidad & Tobago) *The Love Movement Choir*	Ontario Place Island Club	🎵
21:15	22:00	**Magda Aniol** (Poland)	Exhibition Place Coliseum-Arena	🎵
21:30	22:15	**David MacDonald** (Canada)	Exhibition Place Coliseum-Industry (Hall G)	🎵
Thursday – 7/25/02				
14:00	18:00	**World Youth Alliance** (International) *The Dignity of the Human Person*	St. Michael's College Fr. Madden Hall	👥
12:00	13:00	**Groupe Culturel et Folklorique Yaka-lunda** (Congo) *Jeunesse du monde catholique-Maloko madibundu dia catholica*	Trinity Bellwoods Park	🎵
12:00	12:30	**James Milenesa** (USA)	Ontario Place Festival Stage	🎵
12:00	12:45	**Remnant** (USA)	Exhibition Place Marilyn Bell Park-East	🎵
12:00	17:10	**St. Michael's Cathedral** (Canada) *Adoration*	St. Michael's Cathedral	🚶
12:00	12:45	**Vince Nims** (USA)	Metro Square	🎵
12:00	13:30	**WORLD STAGE** (International) *Afaq Parvez Alam, Drums of Bangladesh, La Troupe Folklorique des Chevaliers, Tohono O'odham Nation, Lechowia Polish Canadian Folk Dance Company*	Nathan Phillips Square	🎵💃
12:30	13:15	**Francesca Ancarola** (Chile)	Exhibition Place Bandshell	🎵
12:30	13:15	**Semilla Musical** (Colombia)	Mel Lastman Square	🎵
12:30	13:15	**Spice Island Youthquake** (Grenada)	Ontario Place Island Club	🎵
13:00	14:00	**Conjunto Danzante de Tijeras - Ayacucho** (Peru)	Exhibition Place Marilyn Bell Park-West	💃

Start	End		Location	Type of Event
		Thursday – 7/25/02		
13:00	14:00	**Grupo Rukanas** (Peru)	Exhibition Place Dufferin Bandstand	♫
13:00	15:00	**Hallain Paluku & Alain Mata** (Congo) *Cartoonists/Dessinateur de Bande*	Exhibition Place Café Soleil	🖼
13:00	13:45	**Jesse Manibusan** (USA)	Exhibition Place Main Stage	♫
13:00	13:45	**Matt Maher** (Canada)	Ontario Place Festival Stage	♫
13:00	13:45	**Paléstrina Chamber Chorus** (Canada)	Metro Square	♫
13:00	15:00	**Productions du Grand Large** (France) *Kateri*	Exhibition Place Medieval Times Arena	🎭
13:15	14:00	**Encounter** (Australia)	Exhibition Place Marilyn Bell Park-East	♫
13:30	14:15	**Pinstripe Project** (Canada)	Trinity Bellwoods Park	♫
13:30	15:00	**Sal Solo** (USA) *21st Century Evang-A-Ganza*	Exhibition Place NTC – Hall A	♫
13:45	14:30	**Brianna Dyer** (USA)	Ontario Place Island Club	♫
13:45	14:30	**dAYZ wAGE** (Canada)	Mel Lastman Square	♫
13:45	14:30	**Hope Music School** (Italy)	Exhibition Place Bandshell	♫
14:00	15:00	**Alan Ames** (Australia) *Living the Faith*	Exhibition Place Queen Elizabeth Hall	👥
14:00	14:45	**Ballet de Teresa Mann** (Panama)	Exhibition Place Coliseum-Arena	💃
14:00	14:45	**CAP Jeunesse** (Canada)	Exhibition Place NTC – Hall C	🎭
14:00	16:00	**EnREDados** (Latin America) *Migueli, Martin Valverde, Ziza y Daniel Poli*	Ontario Place Molson Amphitheatre	♫
14:00	16:00	**Equilibrio Precario Company** (Chile) *Mitos de la Muerte y otros Mitos*	St. Michael's College Alumni Hall	🎭
14:00	15:30	**Fr. Stan Fortuna** (USA) *Keeping it Real*	Exhibition Place Coliseum-Industry (Hall G)	♫👥
14:00	14:45	**His Majesty's Musicians** (USA)	Exhibition Place Automotive Building – Ground Floor	♫

Start	End		Location	Type of Event
Thursday – 7/25/02				
14:00	15:00	**Irene Tomaszewski** (Canada) *I Am First a Human Being*	Newman Centre Catholic Mission	
14:00	16:00	**Jeunesse Étudiante Catholique Inc.** (Canada) *Innocent ou coupable?*	Exhibition Place NTC – S103 (Hall A)	
14:00	15:30	**Luis Alfredo** (Spain)	St. Peter's Parish	
14:00	16:00	**Lynn Geyer & John Stufano / ColorBlindMusic Ministries** (USA) *Journey to Forgiveness: The Way of the Cross*	Our Lady of Mount Carmel Parish	
14:00	15:00	**Nick Alexander** (USA)	Exhibition Place Dufferin Bandstand	
14:00	15:30	**St. Luke Productions, Inc.** (USA) *Thérèse: The Story of a Soul*	Exhibition Place Queen Elizabeth Theatre	
14:00	15:30	**Taizé Community/Communauté de Taizé** (France) *Taizé Prayer/Prière de Taizé*	St. Paul's Parish	
14:15	15:00	**Ana Pozas** (Spain)	Ontario Place Festival Stage	
14:15	15:00	**Ge'la** (Mexico)	Metro Square	
14:15	15:00	**Tomek Kamiński** (Poland)	Exhibition Place Main Stage	
14:30	15:15	**Group Gabonais** *chants et danses*	Exhibition Place Marilyn Bell Park-East	
14:45	15:30	**The Rex Band** (India) *The Rex Band Live*	Trinity Bellwoods Park	
15:00	15:45	**Associação Juvenil João Paulo II** (Cabo Verde) *Cabo Verde, seca e escravatura*	Mel Lastman Square	
15:00	15:45	**Cristina Plancher** (Italy)	Exhibition Place Automotive Building – Ground Floor	
15:00	15:45	**Judy Fleming** (Canada)	Ontario Place Island Club	
15:00	16:00	**Rebeka** (Lithuania)	Exhibition Place Dufferin Bandstand	
15:00	16:00	**Tom Booth** (USA)	Exhibition Place Bandshell	

Start	End		Location	Type of Event
Thursday – 7/25/02				
15:15	16:00	**Father Richard HoLung & Friends** (Jamaica)	Exhibition Place Coliseum-Arena	
15:15	16:00	**Greg Walton** (USA)	Exhibition Place NTC – Hall C	
15:30	16:15	**Circle of Friends** (Canada)	Ontario Place Festival Stage	
15:30	16:15	**Sheldon Casavant** (Canada) *The Magic of Sheldon*	Exhibition Place NTC – Hall A	
15:30	16:15	**Starfield** (Canada)	Metro Square	
17:00	18:00	**Daily Mass** (Canada) *Televised Mass*	St. Michael's Cathedral	
18:45	19:30	**Tara Shannon** (Canada)	Exhibition Place Bandshell	
19:00	19:45	**Alonso Sanabria** (Costa Rica)	Metro Square	
19:00	19:45	**Heruvymy Ukrainian Female Quartet** (Canada)	Exhibition Place Marilyn Bell Park-East	
19:00	20:00	**Kelly Pease** (USA) *Teens Journey to Christ*	Exhibition Place NTC - Hall C	
19:00	20:00	**Mark Mallet** (Canada)	Ontario Place Festival Stage	
19:00	21:00	**Sr. Priscilla Solomon** CSJ (Canada) *Rediscovering, Recognizing and Celebrating the Spiritual Heritage of Canada's Aboriginal Peoples*	St. Ann's Parish	
19:00	22:00	**Vietnamese Committee for Vietnamese in Diaspora** (International) *Vietnamese Gathering*	Exhibition Place Queen Elizabeth Hall	
19:15	20:00	**Communauté du Monastère Invisible** (Lebanon) *Ouvre Ton Cœur à la Lumière du Christ*	Exhibiton Place Coliseum-Arena	
19:30	22:00	**Comunidade de Língua Portuguesa** (Brazil)	Riverdale Park	
19:30	20:30	**David A. Vogel & Band** (USA)	Trinity Bellwoods Park	
19:30	20:15	**Dom Dominique Minier/ Splendor** (Canada)	Exhibition Place Automotive Building – Ground Floor	

YOUTH FESTIVAL SCHEDULE

Start	End		Location	Type of Event
Thursday – 7/25/02				
19:30	22:00	**FIMCAP - International Federation of Catholic Parochial Youth Movements** (Belgium) *FIMCAP Evening for Parish Youth Groups*	Exhibition Place NTC – S103 (Hall A)	
19:30	20:15	**Fr. Liam Lawton** (Ireland)	St. Helen's Parish	
19:30	20:15	**Jésed** (Mexico) *St.Therese y Jésed en concierto*	Exhibition Place Coliseum-Industry (Hall G)	
19:30	21:30	**Saint Mary Press** (USA) *Raising a Faith-Filled Family*	Exhibiton Place NTC – S105 (Hall A)	
19:30	20:30	**St. Philip Neri House (Ryerson Chaplaincy)** (Canada) *Rosary & Song: A Rose of Such Virtue*	De La Salle College	
20:00	20:45	**Afro Gospel Chor Paderborn** (Germany)	Nathan Phillips Square	
20:00	22:00	**Alan Ames** (Australia) *Living the Faith*	Holy Family Church	
20:00	22:00	**Associazione Guide E Scout Cattolici Italiani** (Italy) *Europa: Profezia Di Pace*	St. Monica's Parish	
20:00	22:00	**Azione Cattolica Italiana** (Italy) *L' Azione Cattolica perché i Giovani siano luce del mondo e sale della terra*	St. Patrick's Parish	
20:00	22:00	**Communauté des Béatitudes** (International) *"Father, show yourself to the world!"*	Holy Name Parish	
20:00	22:00	**Communion & Libération** (International) *School of Community*	St. Anthony's Parish	
20:00	22:00	**Conferencia Episcopal Argentina** (Argentina) *Encuentro Argentino*	St. Peter's Parish	
20:00	21:00	**Dance Oremus Danse** (Canada) *Wake Up The Mighty Men & Women (Joel 3:9)*	St. Michael's College Alumni Hall	
20:00	22:00	**Emmanuel Community** (International) *"If you believe you will see the power of my heart"*	St. Mary's Parish	
20:00	21:00	**Groupe des jeunes de lumière** (Congo)	Our Lady of the Assumption	
20:00	21:00	**Lviv Theological Académy Choir** (Ukraine) *"Stritennia"*	St. Nicholas Ukrainian Catholic	

Start	End		Location	Type of Event

Thursday – 7/25/02

Start	End	Event	Location	Type
20:00	22:00	**Military Ordinariate/ordinariat militaire-Canadian Forces Chaplaincy /aumônerie militaire canadienne** (Canada) *Pont de Paix - Bridge for Peace*	Our Lady of Lourdes	
20:00	22:00	**NET Ministries/CCO/Life Vision** (Canada) *The Summit - Music & Adoration*	Exhibition Place NTC – Hall A	
20:00	22:00	**OCP - Daughter of God Concert** (International) *Sarah Hart, Susan Hookong-Taylor, Nellie Cruz, Rebecca Harper*	Exhibition Place Bandshell	
20:00	22:00	**Piarist Fathers** (USA) *Evening Prayer and Piarist Prayer (Crown of Twelve Stars)*	Santa Cruz Parish	
20:00	21:00	**Sal Solo** (USA) *Misa Anno Domini Mass: Eucaristía Multi-Media Eucharist*	Our Lady of Mount Carmel Parish	
20:00	20:30	**Tony Melendez** (USA)	Newman Centre Catholic Mission	
20:00	22:00	**WYD Vocations Committee** (Canada) *Celebrating the Call*	Exhibition Place Main Stage	
20:15	21:00	**BDKJ – München und freising** (Germany) *Folk Dances*	Nathan Phillips Square	
20:15	22:30	**Unis-Sons de fondacio – Chrétiens pour le monde** (France) *Unis-Sons*	Metro Square	
20:15	21:00	**Vince Nims** (USA)	Exhibition Place NTC – Hall C	
20:30	21:15	**100 voix du 7e 8** (France)	Ontario Place Festival Stage	
20:30	21:30	**Angelo Paquette** (Canada)	Exhibition Place Dufferin Bandstand	
20:30	22:00	**Celebrant Singers** (USA)	St. Helen's Parish	
20:30	22:00	**David MacDonald** (Canada)	Trinity Bellwoods Park	
20:30	22:00	**Eastern Catholic Churches** (USA) *Akathist to the Mother of God*	Exhibition Place Marilyn Bell Park-East	
20:30	22:00	**John Michael Talbot** (USA)	Newman Centre	

YOUTH FESTIVAL SCHEDULE

Start	End		Location	Type of Event
Thursday – 7/25/02				
20:30	22:00	**NAHUI OLLIN** (Mexico) *El milagro del Tepeyac*	Exhibition Place Queen Elizabeth Theatre	
20:30	22:00	**Renee Bondi** (USA) *Personal Testimony with Music*	Exhibition Place Coliseum-Arena	
20:30	22:00	**Taizé Community/Communauté de Taizé** (France) *Taizé Prayer/Prière de Taizé*	St. Paul's Parish	
20:45	21:30	**Afaq Parvez Alam** (Pakistan)	Exhibition Place Automotive Building – Ground Floor	
20:45	22:00	**Gospel Rain** (Poland)	Exhibition Place Coliseum-Industry (Hall G)	
21:00	21:45	**Dance Oremus Danse** (Canada) *Wake Up The Mighty Men & Women (Joel 3:9)*	St. Michael's College Alumni Hall	
Friday – 7/26/02				
8:00	11:00	**Canadian Catholic Campus Ministry** (Canada) *International Campus Ministry (University Chaplains) Forum*	Newman Centre Catholic Mission	
12:00	12:45	**Danielle Rose** (USA)	Metro Square	
12:00	13:00	**Denis Grady** (Canada)	Exhibition Place Dufferin Bandstand	
12:00	12:45	**Erin Berghouse** (USA)	Exhibition Place Marilyn Bell Park-East	
12:00	12:30	**Gretchen Harris** (USA)	Ontario Place Festival Stage	
12:00	12:45	**Jeunes du Diocèse de Franceville** (Gabon) *L'Anti-sorcier et la Science (danses traditionnelles du GABON)*	Trinity Bellwoods Park	
12:00	17:10	**St. Michael's Cathedral** (Canada) *Adoration*	St. Michael's Cathedral	
12:30	13:15	**Alas del Alma** (Argentina)	Mel Lastman Square	
12:30	13:15	**Luis Alfredo** (Spain)	Exhibition Place Main Stage	
12:30	13:15	**Tim Balfe** (England) *Tim Balfe in Concert – "God is not the thief of happiness"*	Ontario Place Island Club	

Start	End		Location	Type of Event
Friday – 7/26/02				
13:00	16:00	**Comité Hispano** (Latin America) *Encuentro Hispano: "¿Acaso no ardían nuestros corazones?"*	Riverdale Park	
13:00	15:00	**Hallain Paluku & Alain Mata** (Congo) *Cartoonists/Dessinateur de Bande*	Exhibition Place Café Soleil	
13:00	14:45	**OCP** (International) *Bobby Fisher, Jesse Manibusan, Sarah Hart, Steve Angrisano, Tom Booth, Who do you say I am?*	Exhibition Place Bandshell	
13:00	15:00	**Productions du Grand Large** (France) *Kateri*	Exhibition Place Medieval Times Arena	
13:00	14:00	**Sara Torres** (Nicaragua)	Exhibition Place Dufferin Bandstand	
13:00	13:45	**Saruel Music** (Poland)	Ontario Place Festival Stage	
13:15	14:00	**Royal Canadian Mounted Police** (Canada) *Musical Ride*	Exhibition Place Marilyn Bell Park-East	
13:15	14:00	**The Love Movement** (Trinidad & Tobago) *The Love Movement Choir*	Trinity Bellwoods Park	
13:30	14:15	**Francesca Ancarola** (Chile)	Metro Square	
13:45	14:30	**Bruce Deaton** (USA) *Building a Future Full of Hope*	Ontario Place Island Club	
13:45	14:30	**Kelita** (Canada)	Mel Lastman Square	
13:45	14:30	**Magda Aniol** (Poland)	Exhibition Place Main Stage	
14:00	16:00	**Alan Ames** (Australia) *Reconciliation*	Exhibition Place Coliseum-Industry (Hall G)	
14:00	15:00	**Ge'la** (Mexico)	Newman Centre Catholic Mission	
14:00	18:00	**Canadian Catholic Bioethics Institute -Canadian Association of the Order of Malta and St. Joseph Moscati Toronto Catholic Doctor's Guild** (Canada) *Catholic Bioethics: Building a Culture of Life*	St. Michael's College Fr. Madden Hall	
14:00	14:45	**Duc In Altum** (Peru) *Luz en las Tinieblas*	Exhibition Place Marilyn Bell Park-East	

YOUTH FESTIVAL SCHEDULE

Start	End		Location	Type of Event
Friday – 7/26/02				
14:00	15:00	**Eastern Catholic Churches** (Canada) *Redemptorist Martyrs from Ukraine*	St. Nicholas Ukrainian Catholic	
14:00	14:45	**Inés De Viaud** (El Salvador)	Exhibition Place NTC – Hall C	
14:00	18:00	**International Movement for Catholic Agricultural & Rural Youth** (International) *Challenges of Globalization*	St. Michael's College Sam Sorbara Hall	
14:00	17:00	**Jesus Youth** (India) *In service of the Church*	Holy Cross Parish	
14:00	17:00	**Jeunesse Étudiante Catholique Inc.** (Canada) *Innocent ou coupable?*	Exhibition Place NTC – S103 (Hall A)	
14:00	18:00	**Juventud Mariana Vincenciana** (International) *Young People in the Spirit of St. Vincent de Paul*	Our Lady of the Miraculous Medal	
14:00	14:45	**Kairos** (Poland)	Exhibition Place Automotive Building – Ground Floor	
14:00	16:00	**Novalis Publications** (Canada) *Seminar for Young Writers*	Exhibition Place NTC – S105 (Hall A)	
14:00	16:00	**Sr. Priscilla Solomon** CSJ (Canada) *Rediscovering, Recognizing and Celebrating the Spiritual Heritage of Canada's Aboriginal Peoples*	St. Ann's Parish	
14:00	15:00	**St. Luke Productions, Inc.** (USA) *Maximilian*	St. Michael's College Alumni Hall	
14:00	15:30	**Taizé Community/Communauté de Taizé** (France) *Taizé Prayer/Prière de Taizé*	St. Paul's Parish	
14:00	18:00	**World Youth Alliance** (International) *The Dignity of the Human Person*	Exhibition Place Queen Elizabeth Hall	
14:00	16:30	**WYD 2002 Design Department** (Canada) *The Living Tradition: A Discussion Group and Forum on Sacred and Architecture*	Royal Ontario Museum Theatre	
14:15	15:00	**Roberto Bignoli** (Italy)	Ontario Place Festival Stage	
14:30	15:15	**Janelle Reinhart with band One8o and The YRUSH Hip-Hop dance team** (Canada)	Trinity Bellwoods Park	
14:30	15:30	**Jerry Aull (USA)** *Jerry Aull Music*	Exhibition Place Dufferin Bandshell	

Start	End		Location	Type of Event
Friday – 7/26/02				
14:30	15:00	**The Resurrection Dance Theatre of Haiti** *Wings of Hope*	Exhibition Place NTC – Hall A	
14:45	15:30	**Bernie Choiniere** (USA)	Metro Square	
15:00	17:30	**Canadian Catholic Organization for Development and Peace** (Canada) *Josanthony Joseph (India), Mohau Pheko (South Africa): Building Communities of Justice*	Exhibition Place NTC – Hall A	
15:00	18:00	**Communaute des Beatitudes** (International) *Adoration for Life "Child of God, find a new your identity"*	Holy Name Parish	
15:00	15:45	**Dana** (Ireland)	Exhibition Place Main Stage	
15:00	16:00	**Eastern Catholic Churches** (Canada) *The Roots of Eastern Christian Theology: Saints, Bishops & Theologians*	St. Nicholas Ukrainian Catholic	
15:00	18:00	**Focolare** (International) *Interfaith dialogue to build the universal family / Dialogue interreligieux pour construire une famille universelle*	St. Patrick's Parish	
15:00	17:00	**Gruppo "Tintunita" – Pastorale Giovanile Diocesi Di Trivento** (Italy) *Sale della Terra, Luce del Mondo*	St. Peter's Church	
15:00	15:45	**In Ipsa** (Canada) *Famille Marie-Jeunesse*	Ontario Place Island Club	
15:00	18:00	**Novalis Publications** (Canada) *Forum pour les jeunes écrivains*	Exhibition Place NTC – S102 (Hall A)	
15:00	18:00	**Unotone Music Community & Hong Kong WYD Committee** (International) *Chinese Gathering: Sing a New Song – Live Concert of Original Catholic Music, A Celebration of Faith in Mandarin, Cantonese and English*	Mel Lastman Square	
15:00	17:00	**USCCB Young Adult Advisory Board & National WYD Committee** (USA) *Journey to Justice, Peace, Forgiveness and Grace*	Exhibition Place Coronation & Battery Park	
15:15	16:00	**Father Richard HoLung & Friends** (Jamaica)	Exhibition Place Bandshell	

YOUTH FESTIVAL SCHEDULE

Start	End		Location	Type of Event
Friday – 7/26/02				
15:15	16:00	**Jordan Zed** (Canada)	Exhibition Place Marilyn Bell Park-East	
15:30	16:30	**Anthony DeBlois** (USA)	Newman Centre Catholic Mission	
15:30	16:15	**Julie Lafontaine** (Canada)	Ontario Place Festival Stage	
15:45	16:30	**Chantes et Danses de Polynésie** (Tahiti)	Trinity Bellwoods Park	
16:00	17:00	**Emmanuel Community** (International) *Jacob's Well*	Exhibition Place Bandshell Café	
16:00	17:00	**Kante Moussa Pathe** (Algeria)	Exhibition Place Dufferin Bandstand	
16:00	18:00	**Louis & Joseph Remlin** (USA) *International Rosary*	Santa Cruz Parish	
16:00	18:00	**Mouvement Eucharistique des Jeunes (MEJ)** (Canada) *Révéler les 1000 et 1 visages de l'amour*	St. Helen's Parish	
16:00	18:00	**OCP** (USA) *OCP Prayer Jam*	Our Lady of Mount Carmel Parish	
16:00	18:00	**Saint Mary Press** (USA) *Raising a Faith-Filled Family*	Exhibition Place NTC - S105 (Hall A)	
16:00	17:30	**Taizé Community/Communauté de Taizé** (France) *Taizé Prayer/Prière de Taizé*	St. Paul's Parish	
16:00	16:45	**Takillakta** (Peru)	Metro Square	
16:15	17:00	**John Michael Talbot** (USA)	Exhibition Place Main Stage	
16:30	19:00	**Comunidade Católica Shalom** (Brazil) *Festival Sal da Terra – Para os Jovens de Língua Portuguesa*	Riverdale Park	
16:30	17:15	**Daniel Facerias** (France)	Exhibition Place Bandshell	
16:30	18:00	**Eastern Catholic Churches** (Canada) *Eastern Catholics & Evangelization*	St. Nicholas Ukrainian Catholic	
16:30	17:15	**Eric J Sova Ministry** (USA)	Exhibition Place Coliseum-Industry (Hall G)	

Start	End		Location	Type of Event

Friday – 7/26/02

16:30	17:30	**Teatro Renacer de RCC Guatemala** (Guatemala) *S.O.S Un llamado a la juventud*	Exhibition Place Marilyn Bell Park – East	
16:45	17:30	**Tara Shannon & Leah Cogan** (Canada)	Ontario Place Festival Stage	
17:00	18:00	**Daily Mass** (Canada) *Televised Mass*	St. Michael's Cathedral	
17:00	18:30	**Pastorale Giovanile -Diocesi di Ischia** (Italy) *Terra Mia: Emigrazione e Canzone Napoletana*	Trinity Bellwoods Park	
17:00	18:30	**TrypTych Productions** (Canada) *Magnifichant*	Newman Centre Catholic Mission	
17:15	18:00	**Aaron Thompson** (USA) *Aaron Thompson and Soul Pigeon*	Metro Square	
17:15	18:00	**Vietnamese Lasallian Youth** (USA) *Frére Phong & Friends*	Exhibition Place Automotive Building – Ground Floor	
17:30	18:15	**Fr. Liam Lawton** (Ireland)	Ontario Place Island Club	
17:30	18:15	**Hermana Glenda** (Spain)	Exhibition Place Main Stage	
17:45	18:30	**Gospel Myriam** (Canada)	Exhibition Place Bandshell	
18:00	19:00	**Alfa y Omega** (Uruguay)	St. Bonaventure Parish	
18:00	18:45	**Seamus Byrne** (Ireland)	Ontario Place Festival Stage	

YOUTH FESTIVAL ALL-DAY EVENTS

Event	Venue	Transit	Type of Event
Canadian Catholic Student Association &			
Canadian Catholic Campus Ministry			
University Café – Africa 22 July	The Coop Café St. Michael's College	Museum subway	
University Café – Asia-Pacific 23 July	The Coop Café St. Michael's College	Museum subway	
University Café – Europe 24 July	The Coop Café St. Michael's College	Museum subway	
University Café – Middle East 25 July	The Coop Café St. Michael's College	Museum subway	
University Café – The Americas 26 July	The Coop Café St. Michael's College	Museum subway	
Conférence des Évêques de France			
Café français	Medieval Times – South Exhibition Place		
National Catholic Young Adult Ministry Association			
Young Adult Ministry Café	Centennial Square Café Exhibition Place		
National Federation for Catholic Youth Ministry			
Hospitality Café	NTC – Outdoor Patio (West) Exhibition Place		
Scouts Canada			
Scouts Café	Grass – Food Building Exhibition Place		
World Youth Alliance			
Culture of Life Café	Medieval Times Entrance Café Exhibition Place		
WYD/JMJ			
Café	Automotive Building Café Exhibition Place		
Café	Bandshell Café Exhibition Place		
Café	Duc In Altum Café Exhibition Place		
Café	Medieval Times – South Café Exhibition Place		
Café	NTC – Café Soleil Exhibition Place		

YOUTH FESTIVAL ALL-DAY EVENTS

Event	Venue	Transit	Type of Event
WYD/JMJ			
Café	NTC – Hall B Café Exhibition Place		
Café	NTC – Heritage Court Café Exhibition Place		
Andrew Smith			
(Cloudless) Morning Walk	Automotive Building – Mezz Exhibition Place		
Associazione Pier Giorgio Frassati			
Pier Giorgio Frassati Exhibit	Automotive Building – Mezz Exhibition Place		
Centro San Lorenzo			
Centro San Lorenzo & WYD *Cross Exhibit*	Automotive Building – Mezz Exhibition Place		
Communion & Libération			
FROM THE LAND TO THE *PEOPLES / DE JÉRUSALEM* *À TOUTES LES NATIONS*	Automotive Building – Mezz Exhibition Place		
Daniel Tremblay			
Christ's Face paintings	Automotive Building – Mezz Exhibition Place		
Giovani Verso Assisi			
Frati Minori Conventual *d' Italia*	Anunciamo Cristo Crocifisso St. Patrick's Parish	St. Patrick subway	
Government of Canada/Gouvernement du Canada			
Pavillon du Canada / *Canadian Pavilion*	Automotive Building – Ground Floor Exhibition Place		
Jackie Nugent			
Paintings: Our Suffering *Lord in the Garden*	Automotive Building – Mezz Exhibition Place		
Lana Tereshchenko			
My life is in your HANDS	Automotive Building – Mezz Exhibition Place		
Maurice Gaudreault-Diocese of Hearst			
Clay Art Exhibit: *The One Called Jesus*	Automotive Building – Mezz Exhibition Place		
Mediaspirit Group			
Mediaspirit Festival of Media *Productions on WYD Theme*	Automotive Building – Mezz Exhibition Place		

YOUTH FESTIVAL ALL-DAY EVENTS

Event	Venue	Transit	Type of Event
Province of Ontario *Ontario Pavilion*	Grass – Food Building Exhibition Place		🎨
Rosikon Press *"Madonnas of Europe" photo exhibit by Janusz Rosikon*	Automotive Building – Mezz Exhibition Place		🎨
Stanisław Korzepa & Robert Owczarz *Stamp collection of John Paul II*	Automotive Building – Mezz Exhibition Place		🎨
Vocations & Service Pavilion	NTC – Hall B Exhibition Place		🎨
WYD Aboriginal Committee *Celebrating the Spirit*	Grass – Automotive Building South Exhibition Place		🎨
WYD Toronto Exhibit *City of Toronto Pavilion*	NTC–Gallery Exhibition Place		🎨
Zbigniew Nitek *Oil paintings: The life of Jesus Christ*	Automotive Building – Mezz Exhibition Place		🎨
Film Festival	Cinesphere Ontario Place		🎬
	NTC – Tradelink Theatre (Hall B) Exhibition Place		🎬
African Community & Pilgrims *African Centre*	Our Lady of the Assumption 2565 Bathurst St.	Eglinton West subway; 32 bus to Bathurst St.	🚶
Comité Hispano *Centro Hispano*	St. Peter's Parish 659 Markham St./ 840 Bathurst St.	Bathurst subway	🚶
Conférence des Évêques de France *Centre français*	Our Lady of Lourdes Parish 41 Earl St.	Sherbourne subway	🚶
Conférence des Évêques de France *Centre français*	Sacré-Cœur Parish 381 Sherbourne St.	Dundas subway 505 streetcar east	

YOUTH FESTIVAL ALL-DAY EVENTS

Event	Venue	Transit	Type of Event
Giovani di S. Agnese/Comunità S. Martino/Seminario Romano *"Adorazione"*	St. Basil's Parish 50 St. Joseph St.	Wellesley subway	
Daughters of St. Paul *From the Light of the Eucharist to Mission*	St. Stanislaus Kostka Parish 12 Denison Ave.	Osgoode subway; 501 streetcar west	
Eastern Catholic Churches *Eastern Catholic Centre*	St. Nicholas Ukrainian Catholic 770 Queen Street West	Osgoode subway; 501 streetcar west	
Église Orientale *Centre catholique de rite oriental*	Our Lady of Lebanon Church 1515 Queen St. West	Osgoode subway; 501 streetcar west	
Emmanuel Community *Personal Welcome, Music, Prayer and Adoration with the Emmanuel Community in various languages*	St. Mary's Parish 589 Adelaide St. West	Osgoode subway; 501 streetcar west	
Native Community *Native Centre*	St. Ann's Parish 120 First Avenue	Broadview subway; 504 or 505 streetcar south	
Polish Community *Polish Centre*	St. Casimir's Parish 156 Roncesvalles Ave.	Dundas West subway; 504 streetcar south	
Portuguese Speaking Community *Encontro da Comunidade de Língua Portuguesa*	St. Anthony's Parish 1041 Bloor Street West	Dufferin subway	
Schoenstatt Movement *Prayers & Events*	St. John the Baptist Parish 941 Dundas Street West	St. Patrick subway; 505 streetcar west	
York Catholic Community *Prepare to Mission*	York University	Finch subway; 36 bus west	

YOUTH FESTIVAL SITES

Specific Sites	Location – Description	Transit
Church		
Holy Cross Parish	291 Cosburn Ave.	Donlands subway; 56 bus north
Holy Family Church	1372 King St. West	St. Andrew subway; 504 streetcar west
Holy Name Parish	71 Gough Ave.	Pape subway
Newman Centre Catholic Mission	89 St. George St.	St. George subway
Our Lady of Lebanon Church	1515 Queen St. West	Queen subway; 501 streetcar west
Our Lady of Lourdes Parish	41 Earl St.	Sherbourne subway
Our Lady of Mount Carmel Parish	184 St. Patrick St.	St. Patrick subway
Our Lady of the Assumption	2565 Bathurst St.	Eglinton West subway; 32 bus to Bathurst
Our Lady of the Miraculous Medal	739 Browns Line	Kipling subway; 123 bus south
Sacré-Cœur Parish	381 Sherbourne St.	Dundas subway; 505 streetcar east
Santa Cruz Parish	142 Argyle St.	St. Patrick subway; 505 streetcar west
St. Ann's Parish	120 First Ave.	Broadview subway; 505 or 504 streetcar south
St. Anthony's Parish	1041 Bloor St. West	Dufferin subway
St. Basil's Parish	50 St. Joseph St.	Wellesley subway
St. Bonaventure Parish	1300 Leslie St.	Eglinton subway; 54 bus east
St. Casimir's Parish	156 Roncesvalles Ave.	Dundas West subway; 504 streetcar south
St. Helen's Parish	1680 Dundas St. West	Lansdowne subway; 47 bus south
St. John the Baptist Parish	941 Dundas St. West	St. Patrick subway; 505 streetcar west
St. Mary's Parish	589 Adelaide St. West	Osgoode subway; 501 streetcar west
St. Michael's Cathedral	200 Church St.	Queen subway
St. Monica's Parish	44 Broadway Ave.	Eglinton subway
St. Nicholas Ukrainian Catholic	770 Queen St. West	Queen subway; 501 streetcar west

YOUTH FESTIVAL SITES

Specific Sites	Location – Description	Transit
Church *continued...*		
St. Patrick's Parish	131 McCaul St.	St. Patrick subway
St. Paul's Parish	83 Power St.	Queen subway; 501 streetcar east
St. Peter's Parish	659 Markham St./ 840 Bathurst St.	Bathurst subway
St. Stanislaus Kostka Parish	12 Denison Ave.	Osgoode subway; 501 streetcar west
City Sites		
Centennial Park	West of Renforth Dr. at Rathburn Rd.	Kipling subway; 112 bus
Mel Lastman Square	Yonge St. North of Sheppard	North York Centre subway
Metro Square	King St. West at John St.	St. Andrew subway
Nathan Phillips Square	Queen St. West at Bay St.	Osgoode subway or Queen subway
Riverdale Park	Broadview Ave. South of Danforth Ave.	Broadview subway
Trinity Bellwoods Park	Queen St. West at Strachan Ave.	Osgoode subway; 501 streetcar west
University of St. Michael's College		
	81 St. Mary St. (University of Toronto)	Museum subway
Other		
De La Salle College	131 Farnham Ave.	Summerhill subway
Notre Dame Secondary School	12 Malvern Ave.	Main Street subway; 64 bus south
Royal Ontario Museum Theatre	100 Queen's Park	Museum subway
York University	4700 Keele St. Keele St. at Finch Ave.	Finch subway; 36 bus west

EMBASSIES AND CONSULATES

AMBASSADES ET CONSULATS

EMBAJADAS Y CONSULADOS

AMBASCIATE E CONSOLATI

COUNTRY	EMBASSY IN CANADA or USA	CONSULATE IN TORONTO
ALBANIA	130 Albert Street, Suite 302, Ottawa (613) 236-4114	155 College Street (416) 397-3721
ALGERIA	435 Daly Avenue, Ottawa (613) 789-8505	
ANDORRA	Two United Nations Plaza, 25th Floor, New York (212) 750-8064	
ANGOLA	75 Albert Street, Suite 900, Ottawa (613) 234-1152; (613) 234-4550(24h)	
ARGENTINA	90 Sparks Street, Suite 910, Ottawa (613) 236-2351	100 King Street West, Suite 5840 (416) 955-9075; (416) 704-3272(24h)
ARMENIA	7 Delaware Avenue, Ottawa (613) 234-3710	
AUSTRALIA	50 O'Connor Street, Suite 710, Ottawa (613) 236-0841	175 Bloor Street East, Suite 314 (416) 323-1155
AUSTRIA	445 Wilbrod Street, Ottawa (613) 789-1444; (613) 794-2355(24h)	360 Bay Street, Suite 301 (416) 863-0649
AZERBAIJAN	2741 34th Street NW, Washington DC (202) 337-3500	
BAHAMAS	50 O'Connor Street, Suite 1313, Ottawa (613) 232-1724	68 Thorncrest Road (416) 233-6776
BAHRAIN	3502 International Drive NW, Washington DC (202) 312-0741	
BANGLADESH	275 Bank Street, Suite 302, Ottawa (613) 236-0138; (613) 841-3701(24h)	
BARBADOS	130 Albert Street, Suite 1204, Ottawa (613) 236-9517	105 Adelaide Street West, Suite 1010 (416) 214-9805
BELARUS	130 Albert Street, Suite 600, Ottawa (613) 233-9994; (613) 232-0255(24h)	
BELGIUM	80 Elgin Street, 4th Floor, Ottawa (613) 236-7267; (613) 266-2085(24h)	2 Bloor Street West, Suite 2006 (416) 944-1422; (416) 209-1780(24h)
BELIZE	2535 Massachussetts Avenue NW Washington, DC (202) 332-9636	Royal Bank Plaza, South Tower, Suite 3800 (416) 865-7253
BENIN	58 Glebe Avenue, Ottawa (613) 233-4429	
BHUTAN		255 Consumers Road, Suite 401 (416) 498-3150
BOLIVIA	130 Albert Street, Suite 416, Ottawa (613) 236-5730	
BOSNIA AND HERZEGOVINA	130 Albert Street, Suite 805, Ottawa (613) 236-0028	
BOTSWANA	1531-1533 New Hampshire Avenue NW, Washington DC (202) 244-4990	130 Bloor Street West, Suite 1002 (416) 226-2821
BRAZIL	450 Wilbrod Street, Ottawa (613) 237-1090; (613) 294-4530(24h)	77 Bloor Street West, Suite 1109 (416) 922-2503; (416) 713-7809(24h)
BRUNEI DARUSSALAM	395 Laurier Avenue East, Ottawa (613) 234-5656	

COUNTRY	EMBASSY IN CANADA or USA	CONSULATE IN TORONTO
BULGARIA	325 Stewart Street, Ottawa (613) 789-3215	65 Overlea Blvd., Suite 406 (416) 696-2420; (416) 696-2778
BURKINA FASO	48 Range Road, Ottawa (613) 238-4796	133 Richmond Street West, Suite 20 (416) 867-8669
BURUNDI	325 Dalhousie Street, Suite 815, Ottawa (613) 789-0414; (613) 789-7042(24h)	
CAMBODIA	866 UN Plaza, Suite 420, New York (212) 223-0676; (613) 926-6227(24h)	
CAMEROON	170 Clemow Avenue, Ottawa (613) 236-1522	
CAPE VERDE	3415 Massachussetts Avenue NW Washington, DC (202) 965-6820	802 The Queensway West, Suite 100 (416) 252-0660
CENTRAL AFRICAN REPUBLIC	10 The Drive Way, Suite 1410, Ottawa (613) 230-4623	
CHAD	340 Gloucester Street, Suite 606, Ottawa (613) 236-4861	
CHILE	50 O'Connor Street, Suite 1413, Ottawa (613) 235-4402; (613) 598-7619(24h)	2 Bloor Street West, Suite 1801 (416) 924-0106; (416) 368-8574(24h)
CHINA	515 St. Patrick Street, Ottawa (613) 789-3434; (613) 791-0511(24h)	240 St. George Street (416) 964-7260; (416) 419-9839(24h)
COLOMBIA	360 Albert Street, Suite 1002, Ottawa (613) 230-3760; (613) 739-0040(24h)	1 Dundas Street West, Suite 2108 (416) 977-0098; (416) 861-3028(24h)
COMOROS	420 East 50th Street, New York (212) 972-8010	
CONGO	4891 Colorado Avenue NW, Washington DC (202) 726-5500 2 Cedar Avenue Pointe Claire, Quebec (514) 697-3781	
CONGO DEMOCRATIC REPUBLIC	18 Range Road, Ottawa (613) 230-6391; (613) 255-3091(24h)	
COSTA RICA	325 Dalhousie Street, Suite 407, Ottawa (613) 562-2855	164 Avenue Road (416) 961-6773
CÔTE D'IVOIRE	9 Marlborough Avenue, Ottawa (613) 236-9919	260 Adelaide Street East (416) 366-8490
CROATIA	229 Chapel Street, Ottawa (613) 562-7820	918 Dundas Street East, Suite 302, Mississauga (905) 277-9051
CUBA	388 Main Street, Ottawa (613) 563-0141	5353 Dundas Street West, Suite 401 (416) 234-8181
CYPRUS	2211 R Street NW, Washington, DC (202) 462-5772	365 Bloor Street East, Suite 1010 (416) 944-0998
CZECH REPUBLIC	251 Cooper Street, Ottawa (613) 562-3875; (613) 794-2277(24h)	4711 Yonge Street, Suite 701

COUNTRY	EMBASSY IN CANADA or USA	CONSULATE IN TORONTO
DENMARK	47 Clarence Street, Suite 450, Ottawa (613) 562-1811; (613) 236-6292(24h)	151 Bloor Street West, Suite 310 (416) 962-5661
DJIBOUTI	1156–15th Street NW, Suite 515, Washington DC (202) 331-0270	
DOMINICAN REPUBLIC	130 Albert Street, Suite 418, Ottawa (613) 569-9893; (613) 220-7139(24h)	2727 Steeles Avenue West, Suite 301 (416) 739-1237; (416) 835-3273(24h)
ECUADOR	50 O'Connor Street, Suite 316, Ottawa (613) 563-8206; 1-866-204-1735(24h)	151 Bloor Street West, Suite 470 (416) 968-2077
EGYPT	454 Laurier Avenue East, Ottawa (613) 234-4931	
EL SALVADOR	209 Kent Street, Ottawa (613) 238-2939	151 Bloor Street West, Suite 320 (416) 975-0812
EQUATORIAL GUINEA	2020–16th Street NW, Washington DC (202) 518-5700	
ERITREA	75 Albert Street, Suite 610, Ottawa (613) 234-3989	
ESTONIA	260 Dalhousie Street, Suite 210, Ottawa (613) 789-4222	958 Broadview Avenue, Suite 202 (416) 461-0764
ETHIOPIA	151 Slater Street, Suite 210, Ottawa (613) 235-6637	
EUROPEAN UNION	45 O'Connor Street, Suite 1900, Ottawa	
FORMER YUGOSLAV REPUBLIC OF MACEDONIA	130 Albert Street, Suite 1006, Ottawa (613) 234-3882; (613) 565-2155(24h)	90 Eglinton Avenue East, Suite 210 (416) 322-2196; (416) 528-2412(24h)
FIJI	130 Slater Street, Suite 750, Ottawa (613) 233-9252	
FINLAND	55 Metcalfe Street, Suite 850, Ottawa (613) 236-2389; (613) 262-0116(24h)	1200 Bay Street, Suite 604 (416) 964-0066(24h)
FRANCE	42 Sussex Drive, Ottawa (613) 789-1795(24h)	130 Bloor Street West, Suite 400 (416) 925-8041
GABON	4 Range Road, Ottawa (613) 232-5301	
GAMBIA	1155-15 Street NW, Washington, DC (202) 785-1399	18 Old Yonge Street (416) 440-0777
GEORGIA	1615 New Hampshire Avenue NW Washington, DC (202) 387-2390	55 Ormskirk Avenue, Suite 100 (416) 762-8168
GERMANY	1 Waverley Street, Ottawa (613) 232-1101; (613) 797-0472(22h)	77 Admiral Road (416) 925-2813; (416) 953-3817 (22h)
GHANA	1 Clemow Avenue, Ottawa (613) 236-0871	1280 Finch Avenue West, Suite 614 (416) 663-3131
GREECE	80 MacLaren Street, Ottawa (613) 238-6271; (613) 298-8417(24h)	365 Bloor Street East, Suite 1800 (416) 515-0132; (416) 453-3033(24h)

COUNTRY	EMBASSY IN OTTAWA or USA	CONSULATE IN TORONTO
GUATEMALA	130 Albert Street, Suite 1010, Ottawa (613) 233-7237	(416) 604-0655
GUINEA	483 Wilbrod Street, Ottawa (613) 789-8444; (613) 789-3428	702–4383 Bathurst Street (416) 630-4812
GUINEA-BISSAU	1100 Blvd. René Levesque West, 25th Floor, Montreal (514) 397-6905	
GUYANA	151 Slater Street, Suite 309, Ottawa (613) 235-7249	505 Consumers Road, Suite 206 (416) 494-6049; (905) 882-5814(24h)
HAITI	130 Albert Street, Suite 1409, Ottawa (613) 238-1628; (613) 819-78-8519(24h)	902 Bathurst Street (416) 538-3282; (905) 887-9874(24h)
HOLY SEE	724 Manor Avenue, Ottawa (613) 746-4914	
HONDURAS	151 Slater Street, Suite 805, Ottawa (613) 233-8900	
HUNGARY	299 Waverley Street, Ottawa (613) 230-2717	121 Bloor Street East, Suites 1115 and 1110 (416) 923-8981; (416) 923-0878
ICELAND	360 Albert Street, 7th floor, Suite 710, Ottawa (613) 482-1944	250 Yonge Street, Suite 2400 (416) 979-6740
INDIA	10 Springfield Road, Ottawa (613) 744-3751	1835 Yonge Street, 4th Floor (416) 960-4668; (416) 422-3871(24h)
INDONESIA	55 Parkdale Avenue, Ottawa (613) 724-1100; (613) 220-8525(24h)	129 Jarvis Street (416) 360-4020; (416) 360-4023
IRAN	245 Metcalfe Street, Ottawa (613) 235-5105; (613) 852-3043(24h)	
IRAQ	215 McLeod Street, Ottawa (613) 236-9177	
IRELAND	130 Albert Street, Suite 1105, Ottawa (613) 233-6281	1 First Canadian Place, Suite 2650 (416) 366-9300
ISRAEL	50 O'Connor Street, Suite 1005, Ottawa (613) 567-6450	180 Bloor Street West, Suite 700 (416) 640-8500
ITALY	275 Slater Street, 21st Floor, Ottawa (613) 232-2401; (613) 794-1257(24h)	136 Beverley Street (416) 977-2569; (416) 686-9701(24h)
JAMAICA	275 Slater Street, Suite 800, Ottawa (613) 233-9311; (613) 747-5354(24h)	303 Eglinton Avenue East (416) 598-3009
JAPAN	255 Sussex Drive, Ottawa (613) 241-8541	Royal Trust Tower, 33rd floor (416) 363-7038
JORDAN	100 Bronson Avenue, Suite 701, Ottawa (613) 238-8090; (613) 238-8090 ext 24(24h)	
KAZAKHSTAN	1401–16th Street NW, Washington DC (202) 232-5488	347 Bay Street, Suite 600 (416) 593-4043
KENYA	415 Laurier Avenue East, Ottawa (613) 563-1773	
KOREA REPUBLIC	150 Boteler Street, Ottawa (613) 244-5010	555 Avenue Road (416) 920-3809
KUWAIT	80 Elgin Street, Ottawa (613) 780-9999	

COUNTRY	EMBASSY IN OTTAWA or USA	CONSULATE IN TORONTO
KYRGYZ REPUBLIC	400 Laurier Avenue East, Unit 3A, Ottawa (613) 565-7914	
LAOS	2222 S Street NW, Washington DC (202) 332-6416	
LATVIA	280 Albert Street, Suite 300, Ottawa (613) 238-6014	63 Humber Trail (416) 762-6325
LEBANON	640 Lyon Street, Ottawa (613) 236-5825; (613) 236-0032(24h)	2224 Dundas Street West (416) 530-2121
LESOTHO	10 The Drive Way, Suite 1410, Ottawa (613) 230-4623	
LIBERIA	519 Spadina Road, Ottawa 1-877-221-8222	
LIBYA	81 Metcalfe Street, Suite 1000, Ottawa (613) 230-0919; (613) 863-0404(24h)	
LITHUANIA	130 Albert Street, Suite 204, Ottawa (613) 567-5458; (613) 235-0999(24h)	1573 Bloor Street West (416) 538-2992
LUXEMBOURG	2200 Massachusetts Avenue NW, Washington DC (202) 265-4171 3706 St. Hubert Street, Montreal (514) 849-2101	
MADAGASCAR	649 Blair Road, Ottawa (613) 744-7995	
MALAWI	7 Clemow Avenue, Ottawa (613) 236-8931	21 Dale Avenue, Suite 544 (416) 927-7615
MALAYSIA	60 Boteler Street, Ottawa (613)-241-5182; (613) 265-4824(24h)	55 St. Clair Avenue West (416) 364-6800
MALI	50 Goulburn Avenue, Ottawa (613) 232-1501	519 Spadina Road (416) 489-4849
MALTA	900 Dynes Road, Suite 505, Ottawa (613) 226-3288	3300 Bloor Street West, Suite 730 (416) 207-0922; (905) 771-6770(24h)
MARSHALL ISLANDS	2433 Massachusetts Avenue NW, Washington DC (202) 234-5414	
MAURITANIA	121 Sherwood Drive, Ottawa (613) 237-3283; (819) 778-7471(24h)	
MAURITIUS	1485 Blohm Drive, Ottawa (613) 737-7322(24h)	
MEXICO	45 O'Connor Street, Suite 1500, Ottawa (613) 233-8988	199 Bay Street, Suite 4440 (416) 368-2875
MOLDOVA	2101 S Street NW, Washington DC (202) 667-1130	42 Clearlake Avenue (416) 955-9175
MONACO		20 Queen Street West, Suite 3300 (416) 971-4848
MONGOLIA	151 Slater Street, Suite 503, Ottawa (613) 569-3830; (613) 232-2080(24h)	1 Bedford Road, Suite 1 (416) 921-7250
MOROCCO	38 Range Road, Ottawa (613) 236-7391	
MOZAMBIQUE	1990 M Street NW, Suite 570, Washington, DC (202) 293-7146	

COUNTRY	EMBASSY IN OTTAWA or USA	CONSULATE IN TORONTO
MYANMAR	85 Range Road, Suite 902, Ottawa (613) 232-6434	
NAMIBIA	1605 New Hampsire Avenue NW, Washington DC (202) 986-0540	
NEPAL	2131 Leroy Place NW, Washington DC (202) 667-4550	200 Bay Street, 32nd Floor (416) 369-6039
NETHERLANDS	350 Albert Street, Suite 2020, Ottawa (613) 237-5030; (613) 791-0760(24h)	1 Dundas Street West, Suite 2106 (416) 598-2520
NEW ZEALAND	99 Bank Street, Suite 727, Ottawa (613) 234-7158; (613) 238-5991, ext. 221(24h)	67 Yonge Street, Suite 600
NICARAGUA	1627 New Hampshire Avenue NW, Washington DC (202) 939-6570	2351 Poplar Crescent, Mississauga (905) 855-3966
NIGER	38 Blackburn Avenue, Ottawa (613) 232-4291	
NIGERIA	295 Metcalfe Street, Ottawa (613) 236-0521; (613) 236-4719(24h)	
NORWAY	90 Sparks Street, Suite 532, Ottawa (613) 238-6571	2 Bloor Street West, Suite 504 (416) 920-5529; (416) 528-8096(24h)
OMAN	2535 Belmont Road NW, Washington DC (202) 387-1980; (202) 387-1983(24h)	
ORGANIZATION OF EASTERN CARIBBEAN STATES	130 Albert Street, Suite 700, Ottawa (613) 236-8952; (613) 722-2900(24h)	
PAKISTAN	151 Slater Street, Suite 608, Ottawa (613) 238-7881	5734 Yonge Street, Suite 600 (416) 250-1255
PANAMA	130 Albert Street, Suite 300, Ottawa (613) 236-7177; (613) 851-9168(24h)	881 St. Clair Avenue West (416) 651-2350; (416) 483-9719(24h)
PAPUA NEW GUINEA	1779 Massachusetts Avenue NW, Suite 805, Washington DC (202) 745-3680	98 Teddington Park (416) 483-4510
PARAGUAY	151 Slater Street, Suite 501, Ottawa (613) 567-1283	
PERU	130 Albert Street, Suite 1901, Ottawa (613) 238-1777	10 Saint Mary Street, Suite 301 (416) 963-9696
PHILIPPINES	130 Albert Street, Suite 606, Ottawa (613) 233-1121	151 Bloor Street West, Suite 365 (416) 922-7181
POLAND	443 Daly Avenue, Ottawa (613) 789-0468; (613) 565-3068(24h)	2603 Lakeshore Blvd West (416) 252-5471; (416) 606-2643(24h)
PORTUGAL	645 Island Park Drive, Ottawa (613) 729-0883	121 Richmond Street West, 7th Floor (416) 217-0966
QATAR	809 UN Plaza, First Avenue, 4th Floor, New York (212) 486-9335	
ROMANIA	655 Rideau Street, Ottawa (613) 789-3709	111 Peter Street, Suite 530 (416) 585-5802
RUSSIAN FEDERATION	285 Charlotte Street, Ottawa (613) 235-4341; (613) 236-1413(24h)	

COUNTRY	EMBASSY IN OTTAWA or USA	CONSULATE IN TORONTO
RWANDA	1714 New Hampshire NW, Washington DC (202) 232-2882	
SAMOA	800 Second Avenue, Suite 400 J, New York (212) 599-6196	20 Queen Street West, Suite 3300 (416) 971-4848
SAO TOME AND PRINCIPE	400 Park Avenue, 7th Floor, New York (212) 317-0533	
SAUDI ARABIA	99 Bank Street, Suite 901, Ottawa (613) 237-4100	
SENEGAL	57 Marlborough Avenue, Ottawa (613) 238-6392	97 Old Forest Hill Road (416) 782-4676
SEYCHELLES	800 Second Avenue, Suite 400 C, New York (212) 972-1785	270 Brooke Avenue (416) 367-6127
SIERRA LEONE	1701–19th Street NW, Washington DC (202) 939-9261; (301) 365-8076 (24h)	
SINGAPORE	231 East 51st Street, New York (212) 826-0840	44 King Street West, Suite 3005 (416) 866-6134
SLOVAK REPUBLIC	50 Rideau Terrace, Ottawa (613) 749-4442	1280 Finch Avenue West, Suite 407 (416) 665-1499
SLOVENIA	150 Metcalfe Street, Suite 2101, Ottawa (613) 565-5781; (613) 850-0897(24h)	4300 Village Centre Court, Mississauga (905) 804 9310
SOLOMON ISLANDS	800 Second Avenue, Suite 400 L, New York (212) 599-6192	
SOUTH AFRICA	15 Sussex Drive, Ottawa (613) 744-0330(24h)	2 Bloor Street West, Suite 2102 (416) 944-8825
SPAIN	74 Stanley Avenue, Ottawa (613) 747-2252; (613) 241-0542(24h)	200 Front Street, Suite 2401 (416) 977-1661; (416) 725-0821(24h)
SRI LANKA	333 Laurier Avenue W, Suite 1204, Ottawa (613) 233-8449; (613) 747-0844(24h)	30 St. Clair Avenue West, Suite 805
SUDAN	354 Stewart Street, Ottawa (613) 235-4000	
SURINAME	460–4301 Connecticut Avenue NW, Washington DC (202) 244-7488	260 Adelaide St. East, Suite 210 (416) 321-9954
SWAZILAND	3400 International Drive NW, Suite 3M, Washington DC (202) 234-5002	
SWEDEN	377 Dalhousie Street, Ottawa (613) 241-8553	132 Banff Road (416) 489-8438
SWITZERLAND	5 Marlborough Avenue, Ottawa (613) 235-1837	154 University Avenue, Suite 601 (416) 593-5371
SYRIA	151 Slater Street, Suite 1000, Ottawa (613) 569-5556	7370 Bramalea Road, Suite 14, Mississauga (905) 564-0955
TANZANIA	50 Range Road, Ottawa (613) 232-1500	
THAILAND	180 Island Park Drive, Ottawa (613) 722-4444; (613) 863-3506(24h)	80 Bloor Street, Suite 401 (416) 921-5400
TOGO	12 Range Road, Ottawa (613) 238-5916	2323 Yonge Street, Suite 702 (416) 488-5323

COUNTRY	EMBASSY IN OTTAWA or USA	CONSULATE IN TORONTO
TONGA	250 East 51st Street, New York (917) 369-1025; (917) 353-6654(24h)	
TRINIDAD AND TOBAGO	200 First Avenue, 3rd Level, Ottawa (613) 232-2418	2005 Sheppard Avenue East, Suite 303 (416) 495-9442
TUNISIA	515 O'Connor Street, Ottawa (613) 237-0330	
TURKEY	197 Wurtemburg Street, Ottawa (613) 789-4044; (613) 841-5545(24h)	9 Eastlea Street
TURKMENISTAN	2207 Massachusets Avenue NW, Washington DC (202) 588-1500	
UGANDA	231 Cobourg Street, Ottawa (613) 789-7797	
UKRAINE	310 Somerset Street West, Ottawa (613) 230-2961; (613) 230-2420(24h)	2120 Bloor Street West (416) 763-3114
UNITED ARAB EMIRATES	45 O'Connor Street, Suite 1800, Ottawa (613) 565-7272; (613) 778-7277(24h)	
UNITED KINGDOM	80 Elgin Street, Ottawa (613) 237-1530	777 Bay Street, Suite 2800 (416) 593-1290
UNITED STATES OF AMERICA	490 Sussex Drive, Ottawa (613) 238-5335	360 University Avenue (416) 595-1700
URUGUAY	130 Albert Street, Suite 1905, Ottawa (613) 234-2727; (613) 234-2937(24h)	300 Sheppard Avenue West, Suite 302 (416) 730-1289
UZBEKISTAN	1746 Massachusetts Avenue NW, Washington DC (202) 887-5300	
VENEZUELA	32 Range Road, Ottawa (613) 235-5151; (613) 447-4576(24h)	365 Bloor Street East, Suite 1904 (416) 960-6070; (416) 522-8119(24h)
VIETNAM	470 Wilbrod Street, Ottawa (613) 236-0772	
YEMEN	788 Island Park Drive, Ottawa (613) 729-6627	
YUGOSLAVIA	17 Blackburn Avenue, Ottawa (613) 233-6289	377 Spadina Road (416) 487-5776
ZAMBIA	2419 Massachusetts Avenue NW, Washington DC (202) 265-9717	
ZIMBABWE	332 Somerset Street West, Ottawa (613) 237-4388	

NOTES/NOTES/NOTAS/NOTE

NOTES/NOTES/NOTAS/NOTE

NOTES/NOTES/NOTAS/NOTE

NOTES / NOTES / NOTAS / NOTE

NOTES/NOTES/NOTAS/NOTE

Des souvenirs à partager !

JOURNÉE MONDIALE DE LA JEUNESSE 2002
L'ALBUM SOUVENIR OFFICIEL

TORONTO, CANADA

18-28 juillet 2002

JOURNÉE MONDIALE DE LA JEUNESSE 2002

L'Album souvenir officiel
TORONTO, CANADA 2002

18 au 28 juillet 2002

OFFRE SPÉCIALE AUX PARTICIPANTS

La maison d'édition NOVALIS est fière de publier *L'Album souvenir officiel des JMJ 2002*. Cette publication de première qualité, proposée à un prix populaire, regroupera les photos qui rappelleront les moments les plus signifiants de ce grand rassemblement. Y seront aussi rassemblés les extraits percutants des interventions de Jean-Paul II, ainsi que des articles de presse qui alimenteront nos souvenirs pour plusieurs années à venir.

Prix de détail régulier: 29,95 $
Offre spéciale aux participants: 21,95 $
(+ taxe et frais de transport)

Jean-Paul II
se confie aux jeunes

N'ayez pas peur !
Jean-Paul II parle aux jeunes

Sous la direction de
Jean-François Bouchard
et de **Frédéric Mounier**

Préface du
Père Thomas Rosica

Superbe album couleurs de type magazine-
souvenir dans lequel sont réunis l'essentiel des
messages proclamés au cours des sept JMJ
qui ont précédé, ainsi que de magnifiques photos évoquant l'atmosphère propre à chacune.
La deuxième partie est une invitation à décou-
vrir la théologie de la jeunesse de Jean-Paul II
à travers trois grands appels lancés aux jeunes
*"Prenez en main votre vie personnelle et votre
foi, prenez votre place dans l'Église et prenez le
monde en charge."*
122 pages; 12,95 $ (+ taxe et frais de transport)

Memories to share & preserve

World Youth Day 2002

The Official Souvenir Album
July 18–28, 2002
Toronto, Canada

Publication date: October 1, 2002

OCTOBER 2002
2-89507-239-6,
180 pages, 400
colour photos
8 1/2" X 11",
paperback,
$29.95 Cdn/
$24.95 US

ORDER
BEFORE
AUG 15, 2002
& PAY ONLY
$21.95 Cdn/
$19.95 US

This once–in–a–lifetime experience you are a part of will be captured in a lavish, full-colour testimony of faith sharing and spiritual renewal.

Photos from some of the world's top photographers, as well as candid interviews with pilgrims in Toronto from all over the world, will make this a beautiful book of memories to share back home — memories that will last a lifetime!

 NOVALIS

Order now for
SPECIAL PRICE
for pilgrims only!

"Do not be afraid of your own youth, of those deep desires you have for happiness, for truth, for beauty."

—Pope John Paul II

Be Not Afraid!
Pope John Paul II speaks to a new generation, 1985–2002

© 2002 World Youth Day 2002 Journée mondiale de la jeunesse

NOVALIS

Published by Novalis, Saint Paul University, Ottawa, Canada /
Publié par Novalis, sous la responsabilité de l'Université Saint-Paul, Ottawa,
Canada.

Director of Communications WYD 2002 / Directeur des communications JMJ 2002 :
Paul Kilbertus
Translators / Traducteurs : Frantz Duval, Valeria Vitale, Lucia Babini

Cover art / Illustration couverture : Michael Madden – Director of Design WYD 2002 /
Directeur artistique JMJ 2002, Rory Cheyne – Graphic Designer WYD 2002 /
Concepteur graphique JMJ 2002
Design and layout / Conception graphique et infographie : Fortunato Aglialoro –
Fortunato Design Inc., Janie Skeete – Skeedoodle Design
Project Manager / Chargée de projet : Grace Deutsch – Ismant Associates Inc.
Editor / Rédactrice : Anne Holloway

Business Office, English Publications:
Novalis
49 Front Street East, 2nd Floor
Toronto, Ontario, Canada
M5E 1B3

Services commerciaux français et anglais :
Novalis
C.P. 990, succursale Delorimier
Montréal, Québec
H2H 2T1

Phone: 1-800-387-7164 or (416) 363-3303
Fax: 1-800-204-4140 or (416) 363-9409
E-mail: cservice@novalis.ca

1-800-NOVALIS
info@novalis-inc.com

ISBN: 2-89507-329-5

Printed in Canada / Imprimé au Canada

10 9 8 7 6 5 4 3 2 1   10 09 08 07 06 05 04 03 02